# WAR AND CHILDREN

# War and Children

BY

## ANNA FREUD

AND

## DOROTHY T. BURLINGHAM

**MEDICAL WAR BOOKS**

1943

TITLE IN BCL 2nd ED.

# CONTENTS

## PART I

## PART II

The Foster Parents' Plan for War Children has been working with children since 1936 when Spain's children were subjected to bombardments. Later we worked in France caring for French, Polish, Dutch and Belgian children. When France fell we took up our work in England.

More than 20,000 cases of children have been studied by our staff members since our work began; at no time have we had any work to compare with the book, War and Children by Anna Freud and Dorothy Burlingham.

Miss Freud and Mrs. Burlingham direct three wartime nurseries in England for the Foster Parents' Plan. The material for the book was gathered at the nurseries, which are maintained by voluntary contributions from America.

WAR AND CHILDREN is an outstanding contribution in the field of psychology and is as valuable to those working with children on the home front as it is to those working with children in actual bombed areas.

It is a record of children in modern war told honestly and completely, by two of the world's outstanding child psychologists.

EDNA BLUE, *Executive-Chairman*
Foster Parents' Plan for War Children, Inc.

# INTRODUCTION

Work in War Nurseries is based on the
idea that the care and education of young
children should not take second place in war-
time and should not be reduced to wartime
level. Adults can live under emergency conditions and, if necessary, on emergency rations.
But the situation in the decisive years of bodily
and mental development is entirely different.
It has already been generally recognised, and
provision has been made accordingly, that the
lack of essential foods, vitamins, etc., in early
childhood will cause lasting bodily malfor-
mation in later years, even if harmful consequences are not immediately apparent. It is
not generally recognised that the same is
true for the mental development of the child.
Whenever certain essential needs are not fulfilled, lasting psychological malformations will
be the consequence. These essential elements
are: the need for personal attachment, for
emotional stability, and for permanency of
educational influence.

War conditions, through the inevitable
breaking-up of family life, deprive children of
the natural background for their emotional and
mental development. The present generation

11

of children has, therefore, little chance to build up its future psychological health and normality which will be needed for the reconstruction of the world after the war. To counteract these deficiencies, war-time care of children has to be more elaborate and more carefully thought out than in ordinary times of peace.

On the basis of these convictions our efforts are directed towards four main achievements:

To repair damage already caused by war conditions to the bodily and mental health of children. We, therefore, accept children who have suffered through bombing, shelter sleeping, indiscriminate evacuation and billeting. We try to serve on the one hand as a convalescent home and on the other, whenever necessary, as a home for problem children.

To prevent further harm being done to the children. If small babies have to be separated from their mothers we try to keep them in comparative safety within easy reach of their families. We provide every facility for visiting so that the baby can develop an attachment for and knowledge of its mother and be prepared for a later return to normal family life. For the older children we make the necessary provision for ordinary peace-time education and, again, to try to preserve the remnants of family attachments so far as possible.

To do research on the essential psychological needs of children; to study their reactions to bombing, destruction and early separation from their families; to collect facts about the harmful consequences whenever their essential needs remain unsatisfied; to observe the general influence of community life at an early age on their development.

To instruct people interested in the forms of education based on psychological knowledge of the child; and generally to work out a pattern of nursery life which can serve as a model for peace-time education in spite of the conditions of war.

The Hampstead Nurseries consist of three houses, which are financed by the Foster Parents Plan for War Children whose American headquarters are at 55 West 42nd Street.

5 Netherhall Gardens, London, N. W. 3, a large residential nursery for babies and young children.

13 Wedderburn Road, London, N.W.3, a day nursery run for the children from the residential nursery and some outsiders.

Newbarn, Lindsell, near Chelmsford, Essex, a country house for evacuated London children from 3-6 years.

13

The Nurseries, further, give lodging and paid work to mothers while they nurse their own babies, and extend hospitality to the parents of all children.

The staff consists of highly trained workers in the field of medicine, psychology, education, nursing, and domestic science; besides 20 girls who receive training in the various departments. Most of the trained workers are refugees from the continent who have done specialised work in their own countries.

# SURVEY OF
# PSYCHOLOGICAL REACTIONS

All our bigger children have had their fair share of war experiences. All of them have witnessed the air raids either in London or in the provinces. A large percentage of them has seen their houses destroyed or damaged. All of them have seen their family life dissolved, whether by separation from or by death of the father. All of them are separated from their mothers and have entered community life at an age which is not usually considered ripe for it. The questions arise which part these experiences play in the psychological life of the individual child, how far the child acquires understanding of what is going on around it, how it reacts emotionally, how far its anxiety is aroused, and what normal or abnormal outlets it will find to deal with these experiences which are thrust on it.

It can be safely said that all the children who were over two years at the time of the London "blitz" have acquired knowledge of the significance of air raids. They all recognise the noise of flying aeroplanes; they distinguish vaguely between the sounds of falling bombs and anti-aircraft guns. They realise that the house will fall down when bombed and that people are often killed or get hurt in falling houses. They know that fires can be started by incendiaries and that roads are often blocked as a result of bombing. They fully understand the significance of taking shelter. Some children who have lived in deep shelters will even judge the safety of a shelter according to its depth under the earth. The necessity to make them familiar with their gas masks may give them some ideas about a gas attack, though we have never met a child for whom this particular danger had any real meaning.

The children seem to have no difficulty in understanding what it means when their fathers join the Forces. We even overhear talk among the children where they compare their fathers' military ranks and duties. A child, for instance, with its father in the navy or air force, will be offended if somebody by mistake refers to the father as being "in the army." As far as the reasoning processes of the child are concerned, the absence of the father seems to be accounted for in this manner.

Children are similarly ready to take in knowledge about the various occupations of their mothers, though the constant change of occupation makes this slightly more difficult. Mothers of three-year-olds will change backwards and forwards between the occcupations of railway porter, factory worker, bus conductor, milk cart driver, etc. They will visit their children in their varying uniforms and will proudly tell them about their new war work until the children are completely confused. Though the children seem proud of their fathers' uniforms, they often seem to resent it and feel very much estranged when their mothers appear in such unexpected guises.

It is still more difficult for all children to get any understanding of the reason why they are being evacuated and cannot stay in the place where their mothers are. In the case of our children, as in the case of many others, this is further aggravated by the fact that they actually did live in London with their mothers during the worst dangers and were sent to the country afterwards when London seemed quite peaceful. They reason with some justification that they can live wherever their mothers do and that if "home" is as much in danger as all that, their mothers should not be there either. This, of course, concerns the bigger children of five or more.

The understanding of catastrophes, like the death of father, has little to do with reasoning. In these cases children meet the usual psychological difficulties of grasping the significance of death at such an early age. Their attitude to the happening is completely a matter of emotion.

We may, of course, be often wrong in assuming that children "understand" the happenings around them. In talking, they only use the proper words for them but without the meaning attached. Words like "army", "navy", "air force", may mean to them strange countries to which their fathers have gone. America, for the children, the place where all the good things, especially all the parcels come from, was discovered the other day to mean to one child at least "a merry car". The word "bombing" is often used indiscriminately for all manners of destruction of unwanted objects. "London" is the word used for the children's former homes, irrespective of the fact whether the child now lives in Essex or still in Hampstead.

Several of our children in Wedderburn Road used to say in talking: "When I was still in London . . ."

And one boy of four once explained in a London shop, to the shop assistant's great astonishment: "I used to live in London, but

London is all bombed and gone, and all the houses have fallen down".

He was unable to realise the fact that the comparatively unbombed street in which he now lived with us was still the same city. "Home" is the place to which all children are determined to return, irrespective of the fact that in most cases they are aware of its destruction. "War", above everything else, signifies the period of time for which children have to be separated from their parents.

A striking example of such "misunderstanding" was Pamela, a girl of four and half years, who as we thought, had perfectly grasped the meaning of evacuation. She was a thrice bombed child, lived in Wedderburn Road, and like all others waited for the opening of our country house. We had carefully explained to all the children that they were being transferred to the country and the reason for it.

But when at last, after weeks of expectation —because the lease of the country house did not materialise—she stood in our front hall, all dressed and ready, waiting for the American ambulance car to take her out, she exclaimed joyfully; "The war is over and we are going to the country. It has lasted a long time!"

The longing for the Country House, which had been the centre of interest for the Nursery children for some weeks, had suddenly got confused in her mind with the more general longing for the end of the war, which would as all the children firmly believed, take them all back to their former homes and to their parents.

## REACTION TO DESTRUCTION

In this war, more than in former ones, children are frequently to be found directly on the scenes of battle  Though, here in England, they are spared the actual horror of seeing people fight around them, they are not spared sights of destruction, death, and injury from air raids.  Even when removed from the places of the worst danger there is no certainty, as some of our cases show, that they will not meet new bombing incidents at places to which they were sent for safety.  General sympathy has been aroused by the idea that little children, all innocently, should thus come into close contact with the horrors of the war.  It is this situation which led many people to expect that children would receive traumatic shocks from air raids and would develop abnormal reactions very similar to the traumatic or war neuroses of soldiers in the last war.

We can only describe our observation on the basis of our own case material, which excludes children who have received severe bodily injuries in air raids though, as mentioned before, it does not exclude children who have been bombed repeatedly and partly buried in debris. So far as we can notice, there were no signs of traumatic shock to be observed in these children. If these bombing incidents occur when small children are in the care either of their own mothers or a familiar mother substitute, they do not seem to be particularly affected by them. Their experience remains an accident, in line with other accidents of childhood. This observation is borne out by the reports of nurses or social workers in London County Council Rest Centres where children used to arrive, usually in the middle of the night, straight from their bombed houses. They also found that children who arrived together with their own families showed little excitement and no undue disturbance. They slept and ate normally and played with whatever toys they had rescued or which might be provided. It is a widely different matter when children, during an experience of this kind, are separated from or even lose their parents.

It is a common misunderstanding of the child's nature which leads people to suppose that children will be saddened by the sight of destruction and aggression. Children between the ages of one and two years, when put together in a play-pen will bite each other, pull each other's hair and steal each other's toys without regard for the other child's unhappiness. They are passing through a stage of development where destruction and aggression play one of the leading parts. If we observe young children at play, we notice that they will destroy their toys, pull off the arms and legs of their dolls or soldiers, puncture their balls, smash whatever is breakable, and will only mind the result because complete destruction of the toy blocks further play. The more their strength and independence are growing the more they will have to be watched so as not to create too much damage, not to hurt each other or those weaker than themselves. We often say, half jokingly, that there is continual war raging in a nursery We mean by this, that at this time of life destructive and aggressive impulses are still at work in children in a manner in which they only recur in grown-up life when they are let loose for the purposes of war.

It is one of the recognised aims of education to deal with the aggressiveness of the child's nature, i. e. in the course of the first four of five years to change the child's own attitude towards these impulses in himself. The wish to hurt people, and later the wish to destroy objects, undergo all sorts of changes.

They are usually first restricted, then suppressed by commands and prohibitions; a little later they are repressed, which means that they disappear from the child's consciousness. The child does not dare any more to have knowledge of these wishes. There is always the danger that they might return from the unconscious; therefore, all sorts of protections are built up against them—the cruel child develops pity, the destructive child will become hesitant and over careful. If education is handled intelligently the main part of these aggressive impulses will be directed away from their primitive aim of doing harm to somebody or something, and will be used to fight the difficulties of the outer world — to accomplish tasks of all kinds, to measure one's strength in competition and to use it generally to "do good" instead of "being bad" as the original impulse demanded.

In the light of these considerations it is easier to determine what the present war conditions, with their incidents of wholesale destruction may do to a child. Instead of turning away from them in instinctive horror, as people seem to expect, the child may turn towards them with primitive excitement. The real danger is not that the child, caught up all innocently in the whirlpool of the war, will be shocked into illness. The danger lies in the fact that the destruction raging in the outer world may meet the very real aggressiveness which rages in the inside of the child. At the age when education should start to deal with these impulses confirmation should not be given from the outside world that the same impulses are uppermost in other people. Children will play joyfully on bombed sites and around bomb craters, they will play with blasted bits of furniture and throw bricks from crumbled walls at each other. But it becomes impossible to educate them towards a repression of, a reaction against destruction while they are doing so. After their first years of life they fight against their own wishes to do away with people of whom they are jealous, who disturb or disappoint them, or who offend their childish feelings in some other way. It must be very difficult for them to accomplish this task of fighting their own death wishes when, at the same time, people are killed and hurt every day around them. Children have to be safeguarded against the primitive horrors of the war, not because horrors and atrocities are so strange to them, but because we want them at this decisive stage of their development to overcome and estrange themselves from the primitive and atrocious wishes of their own infantile nature.

# FIVE TYPES OF AIR RAID ANXIETY

What is true about the child's attitude to destruction applies in a certain measure to the subject of anxiety. Children are, of course, afraid of air raids, but their fear is neither as universal nor as overwhelming as has been expected. An explanation is required as to why it is present in some cases, absent in others, comparatively mild in most and rather violent in certain types of children.

It will be easier to answer these practical questions if we draw on our theoretical knowledge about the motives for fear and anxiety reactions in human beings. We have learned that there are three main reasons for the development of fear reactions:

An individual is afraid quite naturally and sensibly when there is some real danger present in the outside world which threatens either his safety or his whole existence. His fear will be all the greater the more he knows about the seriousness of the danger. His fear will urge him to adopt precautionary measures. Under its influence he will either fight it or if that is impossible, try to escape from it. Only when the danger is of overwhelming extent and suddenness will he be shocked and paralysed into inaction. This so-called ''r e a l a n x i e t y'' plays its part in the way in which children are afraid of air raids. They fear them as far as they can understand what is happening. As described above they have, in spite of their youth, acquired a certain degree of knowledge of this new danger. But it would be a mistake to over-rate this understanding, and consequently, to over-rate the amount or the permanency of this real fear of air raids. Knowledge and reason only play a limited part in a child's life. Its interest quickly turns away from the real things in the outer world, especially when they are unpleasant, and reverts back to its own childish interests, to its toys, its games and to its phantasies. The danger in the outer world which it recognises at one moment and to which it answers with its fear, is put aside in another moment. Precautions are not kept up, and the fear gives way to an attitude of utter disregard.

There is the observation made by one of our colleagues during a day-light air raid in a surface shelter into which a mother had shepherded her little son of school age. For a while they both listened to the dropping of the bombs; then the boy lost interest and became engrossed in a story book which he had brought with him. The mother tried to interrupt his reading several times with anxious exclamations.

He always returned to his book after a second, until she at last said in an angry and scolding tone: "Drop your book and attend to the air raid".

We made exactly the same observations in the Children's Centre at the time of the December, March, and May raids. When our unexploded bomb lay in the neighbouring garden, the children began by being mildly interested and afraid. They learned to keep away from glass windows and to avoid the entrance into the garden. By keeping up continual talk about the possible explosion we could have frightened them into continuation of that attitude. Whenever we let the subject alone their interest flagged. They forgot about the menace from the glass whenever they returned to their accustomed games; when the threat from outside lasted more than a week they began to get cross with it and denied its presence.

In spite of the bomb still being unremoved they suddenly declared: "The bomb is gone and we shall go into the garden!"

There is nothing outstanding in this behaviour of children towards the presence of real danger and real fear. It is only one example of the way in which, at this age, they deal with the facts of reality whenever they become unpleasant. They drop their contact with reality, they deny the facts, get rid of their fear in this manner and return, apparently undisturbed, to the pursuits and interests of their own childish world.

The second reason for anxiety can best be understood by reverting to the child's attitude towards destruction and aggression which we have described before. After the first years of life the individual learns to criticise and overcome in himself certain instinctive wishes, or rather he learns to refuse them conscious expression. He learns that it is bad to kill, to hurt and to destroy, and would like to believe that he has no further wish to do any of these things. But he can only keep up this attitude when the people in the outer world do likewise. When he sees killing and destruction going on outside it arouses his fear that the impulses which he has only a short while ago buried in himself will be awakened again.

We have described above how the small child in whom these inhibitions against aggression have not yet been established is free of the abhorrence of air raids. The slightly older child who has just been through this fight with itself will, on the other hand, be particularly sensitive to their menace. When it has only just learned to curb its own aggressive impulses, it will have real outbreaks of anxiety when bombs come down and do damage around it.

This type of anxiety we have only seen in

one girl of another age group, ten years old, who ardently wished to leave England altogether and to return to Canada, where she had been born, where everything was peaceful and "no horrid things to see".

The third type of anxiety is of a completely different nature. There is no education without fear. Children are afraid of disobeying the commands and prohibitions of their elders either because they fear punishments or because they fear losing their parents' love whenever they are naughty. This fear of authority develops a little later into a fear of the child's own conscience. We regard it as progress in the child's education when commands and prohibitions from outside become more and more unnecessary, and the child knows what to do and what not to do under the direction of his own conscience. At the time when this nucleus of inner ideas which we call conscience, is formed, it turns back continually to the figures of the outside world on the one hand, to the imaginations of his own phantasy on the other, and borrows strength from both to reinforce the inner commandments.

The child of four or five who is afraid in the evening before sleep because it thinks it has done wrong or thought forbidden thoughts, will not only have a "bad conscience" or be afraid what father and mother would say if they knew about its wickedness. It will also be afraid of ghosts and bogeymen as reinforcements of the real parent figures and of the inner voice.

Children have a large list of dangers which serve as convenient symbols for their conscience —they are afraid of policemen who will come and arrest them, gypsies and robbers who will steal them, chimney sweeps or coal carriers who will put them in their bags, dustmen who will put them in their bins, lions and tigers who will come and eat them, earthquakes which will shake their houses, and thunderstorms which will threaten them. When they receive religious teaching they may leave all else aside and be afraid of the devil and of hell. There are many children who cannot go to sleep in the evening because they are afraid that God will look in on them and punish them for their sins. There are others who receive no religious teaching who transfer the same fear to the moon. They cannot fall asleep if the moon looks at them through the window; there are even children who cannot fall asleep because their fears are busy with expectations of the end of the world.

For children in this stage of development of their inner conscience air raids are simply a new symbol for old fears. They are as afraid of sirens and of bombs as they are afraid of thunder and lightning. Hitler and German planes take the place of the devil, of the lions again in the morning.

In the Children's Centre, for instance, Charlie, four and a half years old, called from his bed in the evening that the shelter was not safe enough, and that the house would fall down on him. He would certainly have called out in the same way in peace time to say that he had a fear of earthquakes or of thunderstorms. Roger, four years old, demanded that his mother come every evening and stand arched over his bed until he fell asleep. It is well known that there are many children of that same age, who, at all times, refuse to go to sleep unless their mothers stand by to hold their hands and safeguard them against forbidden actions. There is another boy of the same age whom the nursery superintendent has to assure with endless repetitions that if she leaves him at night he will surely find her and the tigers.

This fear also only disguises itself as a fear of air attack at night. When we inquire into it more closely we realise that he is afraid that he has done wrong somehow, and that for punishment his teacher and protector will be spirited away at night. We can convince ourselves of the truth of this explanation when we have the chance to remove these children from danger and put them in surroundings where is no talk of air raids. They will slowly revert to their former forms of anxiety. We shall know that peace has returned when nothing is left for the children to be afraid of except their own former ghosts and bogeymen.

This enumeration of the various types of air raid anxiety in children, long as it may seem, is still incomplete. Even superficial observation will show that children do not only undergo and develop the fears which belong to their own age and stage of development, but that they also share the fear reactions of their mothers, and, more generally, of the grown-up world around them. No understanding of their own, no development of inhibitions against primitive aggression and no guilty conscience is necessary for the development of this further type of anxiety. A child of school age, like the boy described above, may stick stubbornly to its own reactions. A child in the infant stage of one, two, three, four years of age will shake and tremble with the anxiety of its mother, and this anxiety will impart itself the more thoroughly to the child the younger it is. The primitive animal tie between mother and baby which, in some respects, still makes one being out of the two, is the basis for the development of this type of air raid anxiety in children. The quiet manner in which the London population on the whole met the air raids is therefore responsible in one way for the extremely rare occurrence of "shocked" children.

An instance of this is the experience a medical colleague had a few days after London fire in the St. Pancras Dispensary. A mother appeared as out-patient with her little girl of five. When asked what was the matter with the child she simply said: "I think she has a cough and a bit of a cold".

When asked about its beginnings, she said: "Being taken out from the warmth into the cold might be responsible".

When questioned further she gave the information, bit by bit, that she and the little girl had been regular shelterers in a big basement shelter under a warehouse. The building above them, like so many others, had caught fire and been destroyed. The exits of the shelter were blocked, but a rescue party had come and dragged the shelterers out one by one.

She said: "As a matter of fact, I have been quite worried about the little one because for a while they could not find her".

It was the transition from this blazing furnace of the shelter to the cold December air which had given the child "the cough and a bit of a cold". We can be certain that this particular child, protected and fortified by

33

her mother's lack of fear and excitement, will not develop air-raid anxiety.

One of our own mothers, a comfortable and placid Irishwoman, the mother of eight children, when asked whether her rooms had been damaged by bombing, answered, with a beaming smile: "Oh, no, we were ever so lucky. We had only blast, and my husband fixed the window-frames again".

Blast, which removes the window frames, not to mention the window panes, can be a very uncomfortable experience; but again, we can be certain that for the children of this mother the occurrence of the blast was not a very alarming incident.

We had, on the other hand, the opportunity to observe very anxious mothers with very anxious children. There was John's mother, who developed agoraphobia during the air raids. She never went to bed while the alarm lasted, stood at the door trembling and insisted on the child not sleeping either. He, a boy of five, had to get dressed, to hold her hand and to stand next to her. He developed extreme nervousness, and bed wetting. When separated from her in the Children's Centre he did not show special alarm either in daylight or in night raids.

Iris, a girl, three and a half years old, whose mother was "quite nervous" since their small flat had been bombed and they had been taken in by neighbours, would demand to be taken out of bed at night during raids and to sit all dressed on a chair. She never repeated this reaction when living with us. We also had an opportunity to observe one mother with a new-born baby who, at a time before the shelter had been built, slept in our house under the stairs. Whenever the whistling of a bomb was heard she would snatch up the baby and could hardly be prevented from rushing out of doors. She must have known that the child was safer under the stairs than in the open with the continual rain of anti-aircraft shrapnel. But this realization did not help matters; it was evidently abrogated by a more primitive fear of the baby being buried in the house. The baby, of course, remained unconscious of the danger but, in watching the scene, we felt convinced that the mother's state of frenzy must have imparted itself to the baby in some harmful manner. Luckily, this particular moth-er was able to leave London soon for the comparative safety of the country.

The fear of air raids assumes completely different dimensions in those children who have lost their fathers as a result of bombing. In quiet times they turn away from their mem-ories as much as possible and are gay and unconcerned in their play with the other children. We have four examples, where their gaiety is of a specially uncontrolled and unforced kind. The recurrence of an air raid forces them to remember and repeat their former experience. Again, it is more the mother's emotion which they may have to live through than their own.

One little boy of four years then re-experiences in detail how they heard the bomb fall on the particular place where the father worked, the rising anxiety when he did not return home at the usual time, the mother's concern over the meal which she had prepared and then, together with the mother, the search for the lost body, the endless inquiries at various official places, the waiting at the mortuary, and the mother's grief and sorrow when the loss was confirmed. For these children every bomb which falls is like the one which killed the father, and is feared as such. One of our war orphans, in contrast to all other children, is immensely excited when he sights any bomb damage, new or old. Another, a little girl of six, transfers this fear and excitation from bombs to accidents of all kinds, to the sight of ambulances, talk of hospitals, of illnesses, of operations, in short to every occurrence which brings the fact of death back to her mind. It is true, of course, that this latter fear is not a true type of air-raid anxiety. It is, above everything else, a reaction to the death of the father.

## REACTION TO EVACUATION

The war acquires comparatively little significance for children so long as it only threatens their lives, disturbs their material comfort or cuts their food rations. It becomes enormously significant the moment it breaks up family life and uproots the first emotional attachments of the child within the family group. London children, therefore, were on the whole much less upset by bombing than by evacuation to the country as a protection against it.

The reasons for and against evacuation were widely discussed during the first year of the war in England. Interest in the psychological reactions of the children receded into the background when, in the second year, the air raids on London demonstrated against all possible objections the practical need for children's evacuation. In order to survey completely all the psychological problems involved, the subject would have to be studied from various angles.

There is an interesting social problem involved in billeting. Children who are billeted on householders who are either above or below the social and financial status of their parents will be very conscious of the difference. If urged to adapt themselves to a higher level of cleanliness, speech, manners, social behaviour or moral ideals,they will resent these demands as criticism directed against their own parents and may oppose them as such. There are children who will refuse new clothes, and hang on to torn and dirty things which they have brought from home. With young children this may be just an expression of love and a desire to cling to memories; with older children it is simultaneously an expression of their refusal to be unfaithful to the standard of their homes. Their reaction may, of course, also be of the opposite kind. The quickness with which they drop their own standards may be an expression of hostility against their own parents. When, on the other hand, children arc billeted on families who are poorer than their own, they easily interpret the fact as punishment for former ungratefulness shown at home.

This situation of being billeted has a secret peace-time counterpart in the child's inner phantasy life. Most children of early school age, six to ten, possess a secret daydream — the "family romance" — which deals with their descent from royal or lordly parents who have only intrusted them to their real, more humble families. Others have secret fears of being stolen from their families and then forced to live in poor and dingy surroundings. On the part of the child these phantasies are attempts to deal with the whole range of conflicting emotions towards the parents. Love, hate, admiration, criticism, and even contempt for the parents are worked out in them. When evacuation occurs at this time of life the fact of being billeted with foster parents of a different social level may be upsetting to the child because it gives sudden and undesired reality to a situation which was meant to be lived out in the realms of phantasy.

The psychological problem of the f o s t e r m o t h e r is evident even to those who otherwise refuse to take psychological complications too seriously. Possessiveness of the mother is, as we know, an important factor in the mother-child relationship. The child starts its life as one part of the mother's body. Insofar as the feelings of the mother are concerned it remains just that for several years. Egoistic reactions of the mother normally include the child. Harm to the child is resented by the mother as if it were harm done to herself. Every human being normally over-estimates his own importance, his own personality and his own body. This overestimation on the part of the mother also includes the child. This explains why an infant who is neither good-looking nor clever may still seem to possess both qualities in the eyes of its own mother. It is this primitive possessiveness and over-estimation at the bottom of motherly love which make it possible for mothers to stand the strain of work for their children without feeling abused. It is common knowledge that only love for children will prevent their continual demands, the continual noise caused by them, and the continual damage done by them from being considered a nuisance.

Foster mothers, i.e. householders, are expected to suffer children whom they neither love nor over-estimate. There will only be two courses open to them. One is to retain the attitude of an indifferent outsider, to complain about the imposition and to try and get rid of the child as soon as possible. The other course taken is to adopt the mother's attitude, which means to feel towards the strange child as if it were her own. The foster mother will in these last cases not suffer from the children billeted on her, or rather she will take the trouble involved as a matter of course, as mothers do.

But this second attitude, which is the cause of all billeting successes, contains another danger. The real mother of the child will suddenly turn up on Sundays or holidays and claim earlier rights of possession. It has been said on many occasions, and once more after the failure of billeting mothers on householders, that it is impossible for two women to share one kitchen. This may be exaggerated. But it is certainly impossible for two mothers to share one child.

There is a third, minor, problem which so far has been less considered. It is the problem of jealousy and competition between brothers and sisters which is presented in evacuation in the new form of jealousy of foster-brothers and sisters. Children never feel friendly towards newborn additions to their family. They sometimes pretend to do so; at other times they are mollified by the smallness and complete helplessness of the newcomer. The newly billeted foster-brother, on the other hand, is very often neither small nor helpless. He usurps rights which the other child is unwilling to give up. The billeted newcomer for his part is deeply conscious of his second-rate position and is embittered by it. There are certainly all the elements for jealousy and discomfort given in the situation.

These reactions are interesting enough to be made the subject of surveys which are carried out by child guidance clinics set up in reception areas and by consulting psychologists attached to County Medical Offices. They keep an eye on trouble in the billets, smooth out difficulties and remove the worst billeting misfits. They have in their positions a unique opportunity to study the situation — especially the situation of the school children.

The Government Scheme for Evacuation of unattended children was never meant to include children under school age, with the exception of some little ones who were taken along with evacuation parties as younger brothers and sisters. Evacuation of unattended children under five was rightly considered a difficult undertaking. They were supposed to stay with their mothers and only to be evacuated with them whenever necessary. When the percentage of mothers who were unwilling to leave London and stay in billets was rather large, a scheme for under-fives was added to the other. These under-fives whose mothers had to have a good reason for staying behind were sent out unattended, either to nurseries or to selected billets. The difficulty remained that vacancies under this scheme were scarce compared with the onrush of mothers who were eager to send their small children to some place of safety.

In a London nursery like ours there is little opportunity for collecting evidence about the successful billeting of under-fives. Children who are happy in their billets i.e., who find a foster mother ready to "adopt" them, stay in the country and little more is heard about them. "Billeting-failures" on the other hand, wander backwards and forwards between London and the country. Some of them may settle down in the end in residential nurseries like ours, which are created either by private initiative in England or by one of the American Relief Funds. More than twenty percent of our cases are billeting failures of various types.

We should be more inclined to hold the billets responsible for the inability of such large numbers of children to adapt themselves to the new conditions if we did not possess first-hand evidence of the difficulties involved from our own observations of the children after their first separation from their families. The most impressive examples of this kind have been described at various times in our monthly reports. It is true that not many children present as frightening a picture as Patrick, three and a half years old, who found himself reduced to a state in which compulsive formula and symptomatic actions played the largest part; or Beryl, four years old, who sat for several days on the exact spot where her mother had left her, would not speak, eat or play, and had to be moved around like an automaton. Even apart from these unusual cases we have seen long drawn-out states of homesickness, upset and despair which are certainly more than the average inexperienced foster mother can be expected to cope with. We certainly see no similar states of distress in children when we make the round of London shelters and find them sleeping on the platforms next to their mothers. Our own feelings revolt against the idea of infants living under the condition of air-raid danger and underground sleeping. For the children themselves, during the days or weeks of homesickness, this is the state of bliss to which they all desire to return.

There are so many obvious reasons why small children should not stay in London shelters that it is not easy to pay equal attention to the emotional reaction of the individual child against evacuation.

A child who is removed from London to the country is certainly removed from a state of greater danger to a lesser one; it exchanges unhygienic conditions of life for more hygienic ones. It avoids possibilities of infection which multiply where thousands of individuals are massed together. If the child goes to a residential nursery, it will be better fed than before; it will be given proper occupation and companionship and will be spared the dreariness of an existence where it was dragged to and fro between home and shelter with long and empty hours of queuing-up at a tube station.

It is difficult to realise that all these improvements in the child's life may dwindle down to nothing when weighed against the fact that it has to leave its family to gain them. This state of affairs is still more difficult to understand when we consider that many of the mothers concerned are not "good mothers" in the ordinary sense of the word. We deal with a large majority of mothers who are affectionate, intelligent, hard working and ready to make every possible sacrifice for their children; but there are a minority of mothers who are neither. They may be lazy and negligent, hard and embittered and unable to give affection. There are others who are overly strict in their demands and make the life and upbringing of the child extremely difficult. It is a known fact that children will cling even to mothers who are continually cross and sometimes cruel to them. The attachment of the small child to its mother seems to a large degree independent of her personal qualities, and certainly of her educational ability.

This statement is not based on any sentimental conception of the sacredness of the tie between mother and child. It is the outcome of detailed knowledge of the growth and nature of the child's emotional life in which the figure of the mother is for a certain time the sole important representative of the whole outer world.

# Development of the Mother-Relationship and the Effect of Separation from the Mother at the Various Stages

In the relationship of the small child to its mother there are definite main phases to be distinguished from each other.

The first phases which comprise the first few months of life are characteristically selfish and material. The young baby's life is governed by sensations of need and satisfaction, pleasure and discomfort. The mother plays a part in it insofar as she brings satisfaction and removes discomfort. When the baby is fed, warm and comfortable, it withdraws its interest from the outer world and falls asleep. When it is hungry, cold and wet or disturbed by sensations in its own intestines it cries for attention. It is certain that the care and attention given by the mother, i.e. in a special atmosphere of affection which only the mother can supply, is more satisfactory to the baby than more indifferent and mechanical ministrations to its needs.

But the fact is that a baby, who at this time of life is separated from its mother, will accept food and care from a mother substitute. Its needs are overwhelming, its helplessness is extreme, and its distinction between one person and another is still in the beginning stage.

Babies of this age who are left with us by mothers will usually have a short time of upset, may cry a while, have more difficulty in falling asleep and show some irregularity in their digestion for a day or two.

We still have to learn exactly how much of this upset is due to the disturbance of routine and how much to the change away from the individual handling and from the particular atmosphere of intimacy created by the mother. The upset caused, is of course, of a more serious nature and of far longer duration in cases where the mother has been breast-feeding the baby and weaning has to occur simultaneously with the separation. Weaning in itself acts on the child as a loss of satisfaction and a separation from the mother in an important sense. When the mother, who has left, reappears after a few days, the baby at this stage will probably not show signs of recognition.

The second phase starts roughly, in the second half of the first year of life. The material relationship to the mother still exists. The mother remains, as she will remain for several years, the instrument of satisfaction for the child. But out of this ignoble beginning of a human relationship something different begins to grow.

The baby begins to pay attention to the

mother also at times when there is no urgent necessity for it to be attended to. It likes its mother's company, enjoys her fondling, and dislikes to be left alone. So far the absence of the mother has only been a potential danger; some inner need might arise and there might be nobody outside to fulfil it. Now, in this later phase, the mother is already appreciated or missed for her own sake. The child is conscious of her presence follows her around with its eyes, can answer her smile and is, as described above, moved by her moods. Its need for her affection becomes as urgent for its psychological satisfaction as the need to be fed and taken care of is for its bodily comfort. Disturbance after parting from the mother will last somewhat longer at this stage.

Babies of this age are sometimes off their feed when left with us. Many show signs of restlessness during sleep and often seem unfriendly or rather withdrawn from contact with the outer world. Smiles, friendliness, playfulness, will only reappear after the bodily functions have returned to normality. This interruption of psychic contact with the outer world is not simply the consequence of the bodily discomfort which the baby experiences; when once used to us the same baby will not cut off its contact with the nurse who handles it even in times of illness.

But at this period of separation it repeats what it did in the beginning of its mother relationship — it establishes personal contact with the mother substitute only on the basis of the fulfillment and satisfaction provided for its bodily needs.

The personal attachment of the child to its mother, which starts in this manner in the first year of life, comes to its full development in the second one. It was said before that the child is attached to its mother; it can now be safely said that it loves her. The feelings for her which it is able to experience acquire the strength and variety of adult human love. This love makes demands and is possessive. All the childs instinctive wishes are now centred on the mother. While she is breast-feeding it, it wants to "eat" her; later on it will bite her, handle her, and whatever impulse starts up in it will try to find satisfaction on her person.

This relationship between small child and mother might be a happy one except for two reasons. The child's demands are too great; it is virtually insatiable. However long the mother may have fed it at the breast, it will express by its resentment at weaning time that it was not long enough; however much time she spends near it, it will still bitterly resent being left alone at other times. Also, the child soon becomes aware of the fact that there are other people in the world besides itself and its mother. It realizes the presence of brothers and sisters who claim equal rights and become its rivals. It becomes aware, sometimes at a very early age, of the presence of the father, and includes him in its world. It recognises him as a dangerous rival where family life is normal. It loves him at the same time. With this conflict of feelings it enters into the whole complicated entanglement of feelings which characterise the emotional life of human beings.

Reactions to parting at this time of life are particularly violent. The child feels suddenly deserted by all the known persons in its world to whom it has learned to attach importance. Its new ability to love finds itself deprived of the accustomed objects, and its greed for affection remains unsatisfied. Its longing for its mother becomes intolerable and throws it into states of despair which are very similar to the despair and distress shown by babies who are hungry and whose food does not appear at the accustomed time. For several hours, or even for a day or two this psychological craving of the child, the "hunger" for its mother, may over-ride all bodily sensations.

There are some children of this age who will refuse to eat or to sleep. Very many of them will refuse to be handled or comforted by strangers. The children cling to some object or to some form of expression which means to them, at that moment, memory of the material presence of the mother. Some will cling to a toy which the mother has put into their hands at the moment of parting; others to some item of bedding or clothing which they have brought from home.

Some will monotonously repeat the word by which they are used to call their mothers, as for instance, Christine, seventeen months old, who said: "Mum, mum, mum, mum, mum . . "

She repeated it continually in a deep voice for at least three days.

Observers seldom appreciate the depth and seriousness of this grief of a small child. Their judgment of it is misled for one main reason. This childish grief is short-lived. Mourning of equal intensity in an adult person would have to run its course throughout a year; the same process in the child between one and two years will normally be over in thirty-six to forty-eight hours. It is a psychological error to conclude from this short duration that the reaction is only a superficial one and can be treated lightly. The difference in duration is due to certain psychological differences between the state of childhood and adultness. The child's life is still entirely governed by the principle which demands that it should seek pleasure and avoid pain and discomfort. It cannot wait for the arrival of pleasure and bear discomfort in the idea that in this way ultimate pleasure may again be reached.

An adult person may find himself in the same situation of being suddenly cut off from all the people he loves, and will also experience intense longing. But his memories of the past and his outlook into the future will help him maintain an inner relationship to the loved objects and thus to bridge the period until re-union is possible.

The psychological situation of the child is completely different. A love object who does not give it immediate satisfaction is no good to it. Its memories of the past are spoilt by the disappointment which it feels at the present moment. It has no outlook into the future and it would be of no help to it if it had. Its needs are so urgent that they need immediate gratification; promises of pleasure are no help.

The little child will therefore, after a short while, turn away from the mother image in its mind and, though at first unwillingly, will accept the comfort which is offered. In some cases acceptance may come in slow stages. Christine, for instance, would at first only let herself be fondled or held by an unseen person. She would sit on somebody's lap, turn her head away, enjoy the familiar sensation of being held, and probably add to it in her own mind the imaginary picture of her own mother. Whenever she looked at the face of the person who held her she began to cry.

There are other children who are spared these violent reactions. They seem placid, dazed, and more or less indifferent. It takes a few days or even a week before this placidity is disturbed by a realisation of the fact that they are among strangers; all sorts of slighter depressive reactions and problems of behaviour will then result. All children of this age, those with the violent reactions as well as those where reaction is delayed, will show a tendency to fall ill under the new conditions; they will develop colds, sore throats, or slight intestinal troubles.

That the shock of parting at this stage is really serious is further proven by the observation that a number of these children fail to recognise their mothers when they are visited after they have "settled down" in their new surroundings. The mothers themselves realise that this lack of recognition is not due to any limitations of the faculty of memory as such. The same child who looks at its mother's face with stony indifference as if she were a complete stranger, will have no difficulty in recognising lifeless objects which have belonged to its past. When taken home again it will recognise the rooms, the position of the beds and will remember the contents of cupboards, etc.

Fathers also are treated better in this respect. The children were always more or less used to their coming and going and not dependent on them for their primitive gratifications. Consequently, parting from them is no real shock and their memory remains more undisturbed. Failure to recognise the mother occurs when somethinng has happened to the image of the mother in the child's mind, i.e., to its inner relationship to her. The mother has disappointed the child and left its longing for her unsatisfied; so it turns against her with resentment and rejects the memory of her person from its consciousness.

## MOTHER AND CHILD RELATIONSHIP IN THE EARLY STAGES

What is true about the small child remains true with certain modifications for the next two or three years of life. Changes are brought about slowly by development in various directions. Intelligence grows and enables the child to get some understanding of real situations, for instance, of the real reasons for being sent way; towards the age of five this mental understanding already acts as a real help in lessening the shock. More comfort can be derived from memories, and hopes for the future begin to play a part.

On the other hand the relations between children and their parents are less simple and harmonious at this time time of life. All sorts of complicating factors have been added to the home situation and confuse the picture when the family has to break up. The child of this age has ceased to live in partnership with its mother only; it has become a member of a larger family group, and this factor has a bearing on its emotions and affections.

So far the emotional development of boys and girls has appeared rather similar; at this age they begin to develop definitely along different lines. The boy begins to identify himself with his father and to imitate him in various ways. This changes his position towards the mother; he ceases to be a dependent baby, and turns into a small demanding male who claims her attention, desires her admiration, and longs to possess her in more grown-up ways. The little girl, on the other hand, has grown away from her complete absorption in the mother. She begins to imitate her in turn, she tries to play mother herself with dolls or with her younger brothers and sisters. She turns her affection and interest more towards the father, and would like him to appreciate her in the mother's place.

Both sexes in this manner have their first experience in being in love. As a result of circumstances it is inevitable that this first love is disappointing. In comparison with the rival parent the child feels itself to be small, ineffective and inferior. It experiences feelings of anger towards one parent, jealousy towards the other, and feels generally discontented that its fantastic wishes to be big can find no real fulfillment.

It acts as a second disturbing factor that the parents use the love which children feel for them to educate the children. The early upbringing of children is not at all an easy undertaking.

Children are born as little savages; when they enter school at the age of five they are expected to be more or less civilised human beings. This means that the first years of life are completely filled with the struggle between the demands of the parents and the instinctive wishes of the child. Already in the first two years weaning has been carried out against the desire of the child and habit training has been enforced. The child's hunger and greed have had to adapt themselves to regular meal times. In this new period the parents criticise and restrict the child's aggression and its wishes to destroy things. They not only train it to cleanliness, they want it to dislike dirt as much as they do. When it is naturally cruel, they want it to feel pity. Its first sexual impulses are interfered with when it tries to satisfy itself on the its own body; it certainly finds no satisfaction when it turns towards its parents. The curiosity of the child is left largely unsatisfied, and its natural desire to be admired is criticised as a wish to "show off." In this first education of the child, the parents do not usually apply compulsion; they simply make use of the dependence of the child and of its love for father and mother. The child is quite helpless in the hands of the parents; therefore, even a slight punishment will frighten it into obedience. The parents' love is all-important to the child; therefore it is used as a reward when the child is "good" and its withdrawal is threatened when the child is "naughty." In this unequal battle nothing is left to the child in the end but to give in and become civilised.

These two factors, disappointment in early love and the pressure of education, threaten to spoil the pleasantness of the relations between child and parent. Whenever the child is denied some pleasure it becomes resentful, when it is too much restricted it turns obstinate. When it is punished it hates the parents; but it can never stand hating father or mother without feeling the strongest guilt about it.

Children are quick in their anger and know

57

only one main punishment for anybody who offends them, i.e. that this person should go away and not return, which in childish language means that he should die. In everyday life at home these emotions are natural and necessary; they create small outbursts and settle down again. The father or mother who have been wished dead at one moment are reinstated in the child's affections in the next. On the other hand, it is probably these violent negative feelings of the child which determine its reaction to separation at this period. The negative feelings towards the parents are meant to be only transitory. Under the influence of daily contact they are held in check and neutralised by the affection for the parents which is constantly produced in answer to all the satisfactions which the child receives.

It does not seem so very dangerous to kill a parent in phantasy if at the same time outward evidence shows that this same parent is alive and well. But separation seems to be an intolerable confirmation of all these negative feelings. Father and mother are now really gone. The child is frightened by their absence and suspects that their desertion may be another punishment or even the consequence of its own bad wishes. To overcome this guilt it overstresses all the love which it has ever felt for its parents. This turns the natural pain of separation into an intense longing which is hard to bear. In theses moods of homesickness children are usually particularly good. Commands and prohibitions which they formerly opposed at home are now religiously observed in the absence of the parents. Whatever might be interpreted as implied criticism of the parents is violently resented. They search their thoughts for past wrongs about which they might feel guilty.

Patrick, three and one half years old, when he heard that his mother had gone to the hospital with a bad leg began to remember a time when he had kicked her, and began to wonder whether her illness was his fault.

Visits or lack of them is understood as rewards and punishments. We had several little girls of three and four who would "hang around" the doors for hours when their mothers were expected to come. But the visits at these times never brought the desired satisfaction. When the mothers were present the children would be gloomy, shy, and hang onto them without talking; when the mothers left again the affection broke through and violent scenes were produced. The children acted as if they could only feel love towards the absent mother; towards the present mother resentment was uppermost.

Again, the reactions towards the father do

not develop on quite the same lines. There are two main attitudes which we were able to observe. The first is that many children will adopt every father who enters the nursery as if he were their own. They will demand to sit on his lap or wish to be carried around by him. A visiting mother will never be claimed in this manner by strange children. The second is that some little girls, two to four years old, will suddenly develop acute anxiety at the sight of any man, will turn their face away, cover their eyes with their hands, shriek with fear and run to the nurses for protection. The first reaction may easily be due to the general scarcity of the male element in nursery life. The second is probably based on the inner rejection of the father due to the child's disappointment caused by separation.

## Further Fate of the Child-Parent Relationship

At the beginning of this chapter we described how difficult it is at the start of nursery life to wean the child away from its mother. It is just as difficult in the later work to try and keep alive in the child at least remnants of its original relationship to the parents.

Most of the children under three will, because of the inner situation described, forget about their parents or at least become apparently indifferent towards them. They shift their affections to the new surroundings and, after some hesitation and some loss of valuable development to be described later, will restart normal life on a new basis.

After three years of age children will not normally forget their parents. Their memories are more stable, a change of attitude takes the place of complete repression. It is already easier for the children to find active and conscious expression for their feelings. The image of the parents remains in their mind, especially when helped from the outside by frequent visits, receipt of parcels, and constant talk about the parents. Frequently, these parental images undergo great changes compared with the real parent in the child's past. In phantasy life the absent parents seem better, bigger, richer, more generous and more tolerant than they have ever been. It is the negative feelings, as shown above, which undergo repression and create all sorts of moods and problems of behaviour, the origin of which remains unknown to the child and teacher alike.

But even at this age where relationship with the parents persists in phantasy, the real affections of the children slowly leave the parents. Again, the child of this age lives mainly in the present. New ties are formed, favorites are found among the teachers and nurses, brother-sister jealousies are transferred to the small members of the nursery community, friendships are established at a surprisingly early age. Pride in the home is changed to pride in the nursery, in toys and all the various possessions of the community.

In our houses, where every possible concession is made to visiting parents, it hardly ever occurs that a child will refuse to leave the nursery with its mother. But there were several small children, about two years old, who showed little friendliness to their mothers when they were at home with them, and refused either to eat or to sleep or to play. They would cling to memories of the nursery — "my bath," "my toast," "my Nelsa" — as they had clung to their mother's name "Mum, mum" — their pet animals, or some belonging of their mother's when they first came to the nursery. The bigger children, three to four years old, know, of course, that this estranged woman who now showers affection on them is in reality their mother; but this rational conviction does not carry them far.

The situation was most clearly expressed in the example of Mary, three years, three months old. Mary was the child who took the longest time to adapt herself to nursery life. For at least five months every visit of her mother was accompanied by floods of tears. Her development was arrested through her concentration on her longing, her disappointments and her varying moods of stubbornness and depression. She entered in July and began at last to settle down about Christmas time. She began to transfer her affections, to be gay and to start all sorts of interests. In January she paid a long visit to her mother and was very pleasant with her for two days.

But when her mother asked her on the third afternoon whether she would rather stay another night or return to the nursery, she said, politely, and sensibly: "Don't you think, mummy, it would be better if we went home again"—

Home in that case, of course referred to the nursery.

Not every child expresses matters so clearly as Mary. But even if the parents are over-possessive and nothing is done on the side of the nursery to fan the mother's jealousy, this situation must be nearly unbearable for mothers with a real attachment to their children. Fears of losing the child completely in this way are often the reason why mothers make sudden decisions to give up work and take their children home.

At the present moment no one can quite define or even make a mental picture of the new shocks of separation and all the innumerable troubles which will arise when, at the end of the war, all these children are deprived of their present homes to which they have become accustomed and are expected to "go home" again.

It is specially difficult to predict how this will react on those children who entered the nursery in the first six months of life and have never had any experience of a family situation.

## NORMAL AND ABNORMAL OUTLETS

It is impossible for children to go through upheavals of this kind without showing their effect in "difficult" behaviour and in variations from normality. Infantile nature has certain means at its disposal to deal with shocks, deprivations, and upsets in outside life. Other psychological methods which are open to adults are not yet available in childhood. Children may therefore go apparently unharmed through experiences which would produce grave results in people of another age. On the other hand they may break down completely under strain which to the ordinary adult person seems negligible. These peculiarities of the psychological make-up of the child may account on the one hand for the astonishing robustness of children, on the other hand for most of the problems of behaviour and symptoms about which all the war nurseries complain.

## Outlet in Speech

Whenever, during the time of 'blitz', mothers came to the Children's Centre after a bad night's bombing, the best we could do for them would be to provide an interested audience for their tales. The kitchen in Wedderburn Road would reverberate with descriptions of neighbors who had been killed, possessions which had been destroyed, and miraculous rescues from burning shelters. We would even risk the children hearing more of the events than was strictly necessary rather than cut short mothers when they unloaded their minds of these horrors. If they repeated the description often enough their excitement would subside visibly.

This most valuable outlet into speech and conscious thought which acts as a drainage for anxiety and emotion is denied to young children. It is possible that they would use this method at earlier ages when with their mothers. Under the conditions of nursery life the children do not talk about their frightening experiences immediately after they have happened. Among all those received at Wedderburn Road after their houses had been bombed, there was not a single one who at that time related what had happened.

The only child who talked freely about bombing experiences was Charlie, who had always lived in deep shelters, and heard a great deal of talk about bombing but had never been himself in any bombing incident. After a period of more than six months had elapsed several of these same children suddenly began to talk about bombing as if it had happened yesterday. Pamela, four and a half years old, related how her ceiling fell down and how her sister Gloria was all covered by it.

Again, four months later, she drew the picture of a front door of a house and said: "The door is broken, and there is a big hole in it."

She knew that the door in the picture was the front door of her former home. At the same time her friend Pauline, five years old, began to describe her bombing experience in the same way.

She dictated letters to her American foster parents: "My house was bombed one time and my bath is broken and my windows. And my pussy-cat was hurt by a bomb and was hanging on the guard, and I picked him off and he jumped on again. And I was down in the shelter with my mammy and granny."

In another letter she writes: "My mammy

and I were under the table and my poor little sister was in bed all by herself covered with stones, and my pussy-cat was thrown away."

Bertram, three years nine months old, was in the nursery several weeks before he could recount in words the event which had been a terrible shock for him: "My father had 'taken away my mother in a big car.' "

The children who lost their fathers in air raids never mentioned anything of their experience for many months. Their mothers were convinced that they had forgotten all about it. Then after a year, two of them at least told the complete story with no details left out. In all these instances speech does not serve as an outlet for the emotion which is attached to the happening. It is rather the other way round. The child begins to talk about the incident when the feelings which were aroused by it have been dealt with in some other manner.

## Outlet in Play

When adults go over their experiences in conscious thought and speech, children do the same in their play.

War games play a part in our nursery as they do in others. Houses which are built are not simply thrown over as in former times, they are bombed from above, bricks being used as bombs. Playing train has given way to playing aeroplane; the noise of trains to that of flying 'planes. Games like these will come more into the foreground after air attacks, and give way to peace time games when things are again normal. After the raids in March and May 1941, the children, three to five years old, repeated in play what they had seen or heard. The climbing frame in the garden was used to provide a high point for the bomber. One child climbed to the highest bar and threw heavy objects on the children underneath. This was also the only time when one of our children was overheard to mention "gas".

A girl, three years old, filled both her hands with sand from the sandbox, threw the sand in the children's faces and said: "This is a gas attack".

This game was played without fear but with a great deal of unrestrained excitement. A war game of a different kind was played by Bertie, four years old, at the time when he still refused to admit the truth of his father's death. He was ill in bed at the time of the spring raids, had a whole tray full of paper houses on his bed and played indefatigably. He would build the houses up, cover them with their roofs, and then throw them down with small marbles which were his bombs. Whereas in the other children's game any number of people were "killed" and in the end everything was left in bits and pieces, the point in Bertie's play was that all his people were always saved in time and all his houses were invariably built up again. The other children repeated incidents of a more impersonal kind in their games; they played active and embellished versions of events which had actually happened. This served the purpose of relief and abreaction. Bertie's play, on the other hand, had the opposite intention—he wanted to deny the reality of what had happened. Since the denial was never completely successful the play had to be repeated incessantly —it became compulsive. The games of the other children remained transitory.

Bertie stopped playing in this way when, half a year later, he at last gave up his denial and was able to tell his story: "My father has been killed and my mother has gone to the hospital. She will come back at the end of the war but he will not return."

No war games are played in the Babies' Centre where the oldest children are now about three years, which means that they experienced bombings when they were less than two.

Dolls and teddy bears are used in play as substitutes for missing families.

Children of four or five still go to bed with

their pets, which they probably would not do at that age under normal family conditions. There are several children who will not be separated from some toy animal which they have brought from home and compulsively hold it in one hand, if possible even during washing, dressing or eating. Lessening of that clinging is usually the first sign that the child has overcome the shock of separation and has found new living objects for his affection. Lending of a toy of this kind to another child is the sign of greatest love between two children. "Mother and child" is played with dolls continually. In observing the little girls, one often feels that the doll does not represent the baby which the child can "mother" but rather that the doll represents the absent mother herself. It is a sign of the greatest enmity between two children when they hurt each other's dolls or pet animals.

S h e l t e r s  are, of course, built out of everything and take the place of what children formerly used to call "playing house."

O u t l e t   i n   B e h a v i o u r

Some children are unable to express what has happened to them either in speech or in play. Instead, they develop behaviour which seems cranky to the outside world until it can be recognised.

With Bertie, four years old, for instance, it seemed for a time as if he were really going crazy. He would suddenly interrupt whatever he was doing, run to the other end of the room, look aimlessly into the corners and return quietly as if nothing had happened. He would distort his face in the most horrible manner. He was restless and excitable, quick to pick quarrels and very worried about his own health; he would not go out without warm clothes even in the summer heat, and so on. It showed in time that this was his way of relating how his mother had behaved after his father was killed and before she went insane. She had aimlessly searched for the father, had expressed her grief in an unrestrained manner, had been excitable and quarrelsome and very worried about the health of the boy. In the end it had been Bertie's falling ill with scarlet fever which had completed her breakdown. Bertie, in his behaviour combined the expression of her emotion, her attitude toward the people around, her attitude to himself and possibly even some imitation of his father who is said to have been specially protective and affectionate towards his family. Curiously enough, these reactions reached their highest point at the time of the anniversary of the father's death.

Another child, a boy of five, has a very definite way of demonstrating the scenes which used to take place in his parents' home. He flies into violent tempers, turns against the people he loves most, attempts to destroy furniture, toys, etc. At the end of the scene he suddenly becomes gentle and affectionate, demands to sit on the teacher's lap and sucks his thumb. His father is known to act in a similar manner towards the mother; he also ends up their violent quarrels with a love scene with his young wife.

With little Bertram, three and a half years old, fragments of odd behaviour are the only means of conveying some idea of his past experiences. He will sit at table endlessly, apparently without eating; this means that he had conflicts about eating at the nursery where he lived before coming to ours. He threatens adults that they "get no pudding"; that means that now he does to others what he experiences in a passive way. At bedtime he "acts up" in a curious way; this was found to be his remembrance of the times when he had been sent to bed for punishment, etc.

Examples of this kind could be continued endlessly. They are instructive insofar as they show that past experiences of all kinds appear on the surface in the form of the usual behaviour problems.

## Outlet in Phantasy

As has already been said, conscious phantasies are used largely to embellish and maintain the positive side of the child-parent relationship. In early childhood conscious phantasies are not restricted to the realm of thought. They go over into action and fill a large part of the child's life in the form of phantasy games. Conscious phantasy in its pure form—daydreams—finds its fullest expression only at a later stage of development.

There is one child who firmly refuses to join in any games where phantasy is used, where impersonations play a part, etc. Bertie gets frightened and anxious when he is urged by the other children to be a rabbit, a dog, a wolf, to play the role of another child, of one of the teachers or whatever the game demands. His phantasy is exclusively reserved for dealing with the tragic story of his parents; it is inhibited in all other ways.

## Return to Infantile Modes of Behaviour (Regression)

Every step in early education is closely connected with one of the phases of the child's attachment to some living object in the outer world. During the first years of life every child should make steady and uninterrupted progress towards social adaptation. It is egoistic and narcissistic at the beginning of life. In the same measure as its feelings turn away from itself and go out towards mother and father, the further family and the world beyond them, the child becomes increasingly able to restrict and gain control over its own instincts and to become "social". When something happens to shake its confidence in its parents or to rob it altogether of its loved objects it withdraws into itself once more and regresses in social adaptations instead of progressing. The advances it has made in becoming clean, in being less destructive, in modesty, pity and unselfishness, i.e. the first setting up of moral ideals within itself, has on the child's part not only been a sacrifice. It has felt pleasure in these achievements because they were made for the sake of the parents and thus brought their own rewards. When the attachment to the parents is destroyed, all these new achievements lose their value for the child. There is no sense any more in being good, clean or unselfish. When the child rejects its attachment to the parents who have deserted it, it rejects at the same time many of the moral and social standards which it has already reached. Most of the difficulties shown by children who now fill the residential war nurseries are due to such regressions in development.

# Bed Wetting

Whenever training in cleanliness is achieved in the first few months of life, it is based completely on reflex action and has nothing to do with the child's psychological reactions. Experience has shown that this early control has a tendency to break down between the age of ten and thirteen months, when psychological factors of various kinds enter and complicate the situation. A second and more lasting control is then achieved by education proper, that is by the usual methods of criticism or praise, reward or punishment within the framework of the mother-child relationship. It takes time before this bladder and sphincter control is purely automatic. During this time the child will be clean or dirty according to the steadiness of its relations with the person who brought it up from dirtiness to cleanliness. A small child will normally have a setback in its habits when it changes hands. When the break in attachment is as sudden and complete as it has been under the influence of evacuation, even older children may revert to wetting and dirtying themselves. The breakdown in habit training is one of the expressions of a breakdown of the mother-relationship.

This history of bed wetting is only one of the many possible reasons for the appearance of this symptom. Bed wetting can be simply caused by neglect; it can, on the other hand, be a complicated neurotic expression and as such only one symptom in the syndrome of a neurosis. But the wetting and dirtying which became one of the main stumbling blocks of billeting are usually not of the more complicated type. Their beginning coincided mostly with the break in the child's attachment, and it often disappeared after a few months when the child had succeeded in forming adequate new relationships.

## FORMS OF GRATIFICATION

In the early phase of infancy when the child is still "all selfish", it turns to its own body as a source of pleasure. Whenever comfort from the outside world is slow in coming or seems inadequate it provides extra pleasure for itself by sucking its thumb. As it grows older other parts of the body, its skin, the body openings, rhythmic muscular movements, the sex parts themselves are used for the same purpose. Under normal conditions of development these autoerotic gratifications play a certain limited role in its life. As the child learns to send its feelings out towards loved objects it also tries to derive its pleasures from them. When its attachments are interrupted it regresses in this respect as well to its former methods of finding pleasure. Thumb-sucking especially is very much in evidence in all the residential nurseries. We can observe big children of four or five eagerly and intently sucking their thumbs as if they were infants lying in their cribs. There is so far not enough evidence to show whether the same really applies to the other forms of autoerotic pleasures, such as rocking, masturbation, etc.

## Greed
Under the influence of denial and regression the child's natural love for food, for sweets, for presents, is often turned to insatiable greed. Demand for affection is transformed back into a demand for material gifts. Parcels from the absent mother or sweets brought by the visiting mother seem for the child as important as the mother herself. This does not only signify that the present can be used as a symbol for the mother; it means that the mother relationship has regressed to the stage when the value of the mother was still measured in terms of the material comfort derived from her person.

## Aggression
Under the present war conditions two factors combine to make children at the nursery stage more aggressive and destructive than they were found to be in normal times. One factor is the loosening of early repression and inhibi-

tion of aggression due to the example of destruction in the outside world. The other is the return to earlier modes of expression for aggressive tendencies. The bigger child then becomes as unrestrained in this respect as it has been in its earliest years. Like a small toddler it will again be loving and affectionate at one moment, enraged, full of hate and ready to bite and scratch in the next. Its destructive tendencies will turn equally towards living people and towards lifeless objects.

## Temper Tantrums

Return to infantile behaviour equally concerns the nature of the child's wishes and tendencies and the manner in which the child strives to get satisfaction for them. Babies can only announce their needs by crying, screaming and kicking; they have no other means at their disposal to enforce the arrival of the desired pleasure. Bigger children can understand the situation with their reason, they can speak, ask, demand, they can alter their position by their own volition, can go and get what they want, i.e. they can actively bring about all sorts of changes in the outward situation. Normally their wishes should also already be felt with less urgency and despair. When a child of three or four sets up a howl because the sweets it wants are not forthcoming or because a meal is later than its appetite demands, we have a right to feel that it is "childish".

The temper tantrums which are so frequent in all the residential war nurseries seem to be the combined expression of the regressive process along the whole line of educational achievement. The children throw themselves on the floor, kick with their feet, hammer with their fists, scream at the top of their lungs and then suddenly turn "good" again, peacefully suck their thumbs or get up as if nothing had happened. It means that they have returned from the sensible active attitude possible for the growing individual to the helpless and despairing passivity of their infant stage.

## Abnormal Withdrawal of the Emotional Interest from the Outside World

With our present experience we expect the state of homesickness to last any length of time from a few hours to several weeks or even a few months. When this period is over the child finds itself attached to new people in its new surroundings. The new ties may be less solid and more superficial than the original ones. As already described, the child starts its new relationships on a more primitive level, and some valuable achievements are lost during the process of adaptation. But however big or small that loss may be, the fact remains that normally the withdrawal of emotional interest will be temporary and the child will return sooner or later to good relations with the outside world. It is different in cases where, through a series of unlucky circumstances, the child has to change hands more than once or twice so that its new attachments are again wasted, and it is deprived of its new objects as soon as they are found. Its relations to people will then become more and more superficial and abnormal reactions of some kind will certainly follow. We were able to observe two cases of this kind.

Johnny had changed his place of living several times between the age of two and three, He had never been separated from his mother up to the age of two, and spent 14 months of that time alone with her after father had been drafted into the army. His wanderings began when his mother fell ill with tuberculosis and went into a hospital. She once returned from the hospital because she heard that he was unhappy in the place where she had left him. She took him home to her relatives in the hope that she would be able to leave him there. Since all her sisters had gone out on war work there was nobody to leave him with, and she again found a private billet in the country. She left him there to return to the hospital. In the meantime he had developed bed wetting so that the billet would not keep him. Again he began to wander until he landed in our country house at the age of three. Observations showed that as a result of his experiences he had become completely and frighteningly impersonal. His face, though very good looking, was expressionless; a stereotyped smile would appear at times. He was neither shy nor forward, ready to stay where he was put and did not seem afraid of the new surroundings. He made no distinction between one grown-up and another, clung to no one and avoided no one. He ate, slept and played and was no trouble to anybody; the only abnormal feature about him was that he seemed completely devoid of all emotion. For several weeks it was very difficult to get nearer to him in any way. The ice was broken at last when he fell ill and was isolated with one nurse. Whenever his temperature was taken the nurse held him on her lap and put her arm around his shoulders to keep the thermometer in place. Until then he had been indifferent to every kind of fondling; this special position evidently aroused in him memories of being in his mother's arms. He became attached to the nurse, asked repeatedly for "his temperchure" and found the way back to his feelings with the help of this incident.

The second case, Sylvia, three and a half years old, showed even worse abnormality. She holds the record with six different billets between the age of two and three. Her parents are highly skilled war workers who sent her to the country at the beginning of the war with her older sisters' evacuation school party. She was unhappy in some billets, not well treated in others, and had to leave one place after the other because her foster mothers fell ill, went to hospital etc. In the end she became completely confused and failed to recognise her own mother though both parents visited in turns nearly fortnightly. Her emotional withdrawal from the outside world was the same as Johnny's, all her other reactions were exactly opposite. Where Johnny showed complete lack of emotion she had emotional outbreaks of an hysterical type—fits of crying alternated with fits of laughing. Where Johnny was easy to handle, she was impossible. When she came to our nursery she would not go to bed, could not sleep, would not eat, fought against being bathed, washed, dressed or undressed. She had fears of going downstairs, of leaving the house, of entering again through the front door. Sometimes she would like to play with other children, at other times she screamed with fear when they approached her. When she returns from a visit to her parents' home where she is now sent regularly, she tells phantastic tales about the events which happen there. Everybody pushes everybody else, her sisters hit her on the head, she is pushed into the fire and everything burns up. There are no bombing experiences at the root of Sylvia's fears. She is one among the few of our children who escaped the London air raids through early evacuation to the country.

As a consequence of the shock of her repeated separations she has developed a neurotic illness which is so far difficult to diagnose. Hysterical symptoms alternate with phobic behaviour and compulsive mechanisms. The main feature is her withdrawal from the interests of the real outer world. Her expression is always worried, her glance fixed and stony. There is little hope that, like Johnny, she will find a natural return to normality. She is ill enough to need and receive psycho-analytical treatment for her neurosis.

## PRACTICAL CONCLUSIONS

At first glance it seems from this material as if small children had little chance to escape unharmed from the present war conditions. They either stay in the bombed areas with their parents and, quite apart from physical danger, get upset by their mothers' fears and excitements, and hardened and brutalised by the destruction which goes on around them and by shelter life. Or else they avoid these dangers, are evacuated to the country and suffer other shocks through separation from the parents at an age which needs emotional stability and permanency. Choosing between two evils seems to be all that war-time care is able to accomplish for them.

On the other hand we should not be too quick in drawing such conclusions. That evacuation under the present conditions is as upsetting as bombing itself is no proof yet that methods of evacuation could not be found which guard the children's life and bodily health and at the same time provide the possibility for normal psychological development and steady progress in education.

Our case material shows that it is not so much the fact of separation to which the child reacts abnormally as the form in which the separation has taken place. The child experiences shock when it is suddenly and without preparation exposed to dangers with which it cannot cope emotionally. In the case of evacuation the danger is represented by the sudden disappearance of all the people whom it knows and loves. Unsatisfied longing produces in it a state of tension which is felt as shock. If separation happened slowly, if the people who are meant to substitute for the mother were known to the child beforehand, transition from one object to the other would proceed gradually. If the mother reappeared several times during the period when the child had to be weaned from her, the pain of separation would be repeated, but it would be felt each successive time in smaller doses. By the time the affection of the child had let go of the mother the new substitute object would be well known and ready at hand. There would be no empty period in which the feelings of the child are turned completely inward and, consequently, there would be little loss of educational achievement. Regression occurs while the child is passing through the no-man's-land of affection, i.e. during the time the old object has been given up and before the new one has been found. Two of our children have expressed this state of mind in their own words.

Bertram, three and three-quarters years old, said: "I don't like you, I don't like anybody! I only like myself". Ivan, five years old, exclaimed: "I am nobody's nothing".

Mothers are commonly advised not to visit their children during the first fortnight after separation. It is the common opinion that the pain of separation will then pass more quickly and cause less disturbance. In reality it is the very quickness of the child's break with the mother which contains all the dangers of abnormal consequences. Long drawn-out separation may bring more visible pain but it is less harmful because it gives the child time to accompany the events with his reactions, to work through his own feelings over and over again, to find outward expressions for his state of mind, i.e. to abreact slowly. Reactions which do not even reach the child's consciousness can do incalculable harm to its normality.

Objection might be raised that emergency war conditions do not allow considerations of this kind to carry weight. Still, it seems possible to base plans for "evacuation in slow stages" on psychological convictions of this kind.

If children under five have to be evacuated, unattended like their bigger brothers and sisters they should at least not be sent out under harder conditions than the older ones. School children, even if they lose the connection with their homes, will at least retain the relationship to their school friends and to their teachers who go out with them. Under-fives who are sent to nurseries go into the complete unknown.

One could conceive a plan under which all small children would be collected in day nurseries. They would get attached to their nurses and teachers and know the units in which they spend their days while they still live at home. In times of danger these day nurseries would be converted into residential nurseries and would be evacuated collectively. Mothers who refuse to part from their small children could be offered the chance to go too as paid domestic staff. Experience has shown that only a small percentage of all mothers would choose to do so. Under such conditions evacuation would lose its horrors for the young child and abnormal reactions to it would become extremely rare. To maintain the remnants of the parent relationship as far as possible and simultaneously to prepare the way for the return of children to their homes after the war, there should be little or no restriction of visiting rules. In our houses parents come and go whenever their occupations leave them free to do so. Provision should be made for the possibility of such visits, as it is made for all the other bodily and educational needs of the child insofar as they are considered to be important.

It will be still harder to devise proper means of evacuation for small babies. If infants have to be separated from their mothers in the first weeks of life in the interest of war work, it is best they go to creches near factories where mothers can deposit and collect them. This again does not solve the problem of shelter sleeping in times of danger. If babies go to residential homes these should be situated as near to the outskirts of the town as possible to encourage frequent visiting. With infants there are no "remnants of a mother relationship" to maintain, and no memories to keep alive. The baby will have to make the acquaintance of his mother during the hours or days of visiting. There should certainly be some relation between the frequency of visits and the ability reached by the infant to retain remembrance.

# REPORTS

The previous part of the book is based on case-history notes drawn from daily contact with a living, war-time laboratory. The succeeding reports give the reader an opportunity to follow intimately the events as they occurred and thus see how Anna Freud and Dorothy Burlingham reached their conclusions.

## HAMPSTEAD NURSERY

In day-time the life of the children does not differ in any way from that of an institution under peace-time conditions. The children play, paint, draw, sing, dance in the nurseries; go for walks in the street or play in our garden where they learn climbing on a jungle gym. We disregard day-light raids except for calling the children in from the garden or the street when the sirens go on. Londoners otherwise ignore day-light raids except when a plane is heard directly overhead. But it is thought best to keep children home during raids as much as possible, to avoid the chance of their being hit by odd pieces of shrapnel.

Every evening, whether there is an air-raid or not, the children are settled down in their shelter beds, the shelter taking the place of an ordinary bed-room. This is much wiser than putting the children to bed upstairs and only taking them to shelter when the sirens go. The routine of their waking and sleeping remains in this way independent of air-raids and lulls. They go to bed at their usual time and there is no need to disturb them when hostilities begin outside.

## Allaying Fear

Even children whose mothers claimed that they had been badly frightened by raids showed, surprisingly enough, little interest in sirens, bombs, guns or "all clears."

A girl of four years suggested to the kindergarten teacher who was trying to quiet a noisy child in his shelter bed that, if he would not promise to be good, she should "take him upstairs to a danger-room".

A little girl of three and a half years, being asked whether she was pleased to see a visiting uncle, says crossly: "No, I want him bombed."

Our big girls, six and nine years old, when we take them for a walk and pass by damaged houses make expert casual remarks: "Incendiary bomb". This is where the roof is burned out. "High explosive". This is where the walls are badly shaken.

The same two girls tell about the time when they still lived with their parents in a badly bombed area: "Every evening when the first bombs came down, Daddy would grab his coat and run out to help and mummy would always call after him: 'Don't forget that we have two spare beds and bring in people if you find them homeless'."

Children whose parents behave in that way, naturally show no sign of fear themselves.

The father says of the six year old girl:

"You would have to drop a bomb down her back before she would take notice!"

It is different with the two of our children who were brought in by excessively nervous mothers, women who had developed states of grave anxiety after having been bombed, one at home and one in a shelter. Those mothers used to pull their children out of bed and stand around trembling; one child stood near his mother all night, unable to leave her. They naturally imparted their own fears to their children. But even these children, after the separation from their mothers, quickly lose their state of tension and settle down to ordinary life.

### Parent Co-operation

We were warned in the beginning that we would find the London parents of the poorer classes to be rather unappreciative, critical and only too glad to dump their children on us and forget all about them and their further obligations. What we experience is exactly the opposite. With the exception of three mothers whom one can hardly regard as responsible personalities, one can only admire the efforts which the parents make for their children under the worst possible conditions, their attempts at co-operation with us and their real delight at every chance which is offered to their children. They appreciate every improvement in health, weight or the happiness of the child.

Parents of this class are used to obeying hospital rules regarding visiting. They are surprised and delighted when they hear that we are glad to have them come at any time. If their occupation allows, they can come freely to take their children out for walks, bathe them, put them to bed in the evening, and share their meals without any undue interference with our household routine. In practice this only happens during week-ends when our home sometimes takes on the character of a coffee house, club or restaurant.

It is true that in this way children take a longer time to get over the separation from their parents and the repeated "separations" after visiting days are often followed by outburst of crying and violent emotions. But we consider this slower method of overcoming the shock of separation as much less harmful to the child than the traumatic one usual in evacuation when many little children who have never been away from their mothers for a single night, are suddenly taken from them, not to see them again for weeks or even months.

# THE SHOCK OF SEPARATION

Life in London has been greatly influenced by the fact that bombing was less regular and that there was even a long succession of quiet nights. The very few bad air-raids that occurred did no damage in the immediate neighborhood of the Nursery.

Since darkness comes later, the children are usually asleep now before any noise is to be heard. The exception was one evening raid when noise of terrific anti-aircraft fire struck the children at the time of settling down to sleep. There was one child only, Charlie, four and a half years old, who showed genuine signs of anxiety. Pauline, four and a half years old, who usually adopts a motherly attitude towards him as a playmate, advised him to "cover himself right over" as she always did in such cases. All other children did not seem to pay overmuch attention either to the danger or to Charlie's state of anxiety.

It may be interesting to note in this respect that Charlie, who is the child most easily worried about war dangers, is one of the few children in the house who has not been through the experience of being actually bombed. Pauline on the other hand is one of the "bombed" children. A bomb which fell in the street next to the one in which she lived with her mother and grandmother took off the roof of her house and destroyed the attic room from which the family had just escaped downstairs a few seconds before.

With other children also over-sensitiveness to danger seems to have nothing to do with the actual experience of bombing which has gone before. We can still only see that the children's fears are to a large extent dependent on their parents' anxieties wherever it is existent. After separation from those parents, fears either vanish or decrease. Anxiety of playmates does not seem to be infectious in the same sense.

A closer examination of the applications received shows that the children most physically endangered by the present state of affairs are those up to two years of age. It is easy to understand that infants simply cannot live in a state of emergency. The same conditions which to the fully developed individual only mean a passing state of discomfort of body or mind are capable of completely arresting or seriously damaging the development of the growing human being. The younger and more undeveloped the individual the more serious the consequences. We have, after all, always known that development demands its own conditions, irrespective of war and peace or all other happenings in the outer world.

# Patrick

Patrick, a boy of three years and two months, of pleasing appearance, well built and rather big for his age, was sent to us after one unsuccessful attempt at evacuation to the country. In the billet where he had been placed, he had, as the report stated, "fretted" so much for his mother that he was sent back to her after a very few days. Unluckily their reunion was of short duration. He contracted measles and had to suffer another enforced separation from his mother. After dismissal from hospital she brought him directly to us since she had been warned not to take him after illness to the Tube station where she herself was sleeping regularly with her husband. She admonished him to be "a good boy", and promised to visit him if he would promise not to cry for her.

The state of affairs that devleoped after she left was a most unhappy one. Patrick tried to keep his promise and was not seen crying. Instead he would nod his head whenever anyone l o o k e d at him and assured himself and anybody who cared to listen with the greatest show of confidence that his mother would come for him, that she would put on his overcoat and would take him home with her again. Whenever a listener seemed to believe him he was satisfied; whenever anybody contradicted him, he would burst into violent tears.

This same state of affairs continued through the next two or three days with several additions. The nodding took on a more compulsive and automatic character: "My mother will put on my overcoat and take me home again."

Later an ever growing list of clothes that his mother was supposed to put on him was added: "She will put on my overcoat and my leggings, she will zip up the zipper, she will put on my pixie hat."

When the repetitions of this formula became monotonous and endless, somebody asked him whether he could not stop saying it all over again. Again Patrick tried to be the good boy that his mother wanted him to be. He stopped repeating the formula aloud but his moving lips showed that he was saying it over and over to himself.

At the same time he substituted for the spoken words gestures that showed the position of his pixie hat, the putting on of an imaginary coat, the zipping of the zipper etc. What showed as an expressive movement one day, was reduced the next to a mere abortive flicker of his fingers. While the other children were mostly busy with their toys, playing games, making music etc., Patrick, totally uninterested, would stand somewhere in a corner, move his hands and lips with an absolutely tragic expression on his face. These movements also would not stop when he was dressing or eating, going up or downstairs. He refused most kinds of food but would drink milk plentifully.

We were shocked to see an apparently healthy child develop a compulsive tie under our very eyes. All attempts to get in contact with him were unsatisfactory. Not that it was impossible to break in on his compulsive behaviour with understanding words, affection and sympathy. But in such moments, instead of reiterating his false assurances, he would break through to the truth, burst into tears and develop an excess of grief that one felt at a loss how to meet.

From the second day on we had made attempts to reach his mother and induce her to visit him regularly. Unluckily again she had fallen ill with a bad influenza and was lying in a hospital. A Sunday afternoon visit from his father did not bring the slightest comfort. It took more than a week before his mother was dismissed from the hospital. She came immediately to us. We discussed the situation with her and persuaded her to stay in our house for a while.

The aspect of Patrick's state changed immediately. He dropped his symptom and instead clung to his mother with the utmost tenacity. For several days and nights he would hardly leave her side. Whenever she went upstairs or downstairs, Patrick was trailing after her. Whenever she disappeared for a minute we could hear his anxious questioning through the house, or see him open the door of every room and look searchingly into every corner. No one was allowed to touch him, his mother bathed him, put him to sleep and had her shelter bed next to his.

A few days were sufficient to do away also with this abnormal state of affairs. Slowly Patrick lost his excessive clinging and turned at times to the other children to join in their play. His mother was first allowed to go home for an hour to cook a meal for his father. He would wait anxiously for her reappearance and signs of the former anxiety would show in his expression. But after a further week or two these symptoms also disappeared. Patrick's mother was allowed to come and go freely and Patrick became a member of the Nursery like any other child.

At the present time he is one of the most active children in the playroom; his rather girlish mannerisms having changed to definitely boyish behaviour. He jumps and climbs, is very good at building and keeps busy from morning till night. He is a very good eater, only satisfied after repeated helpings.

After some consideration, we offered the mother, who is an unusually fine woman and has at some former time been employed as charwoman in a day Nursery, the paid post of emergency night nurse in our two shelters. That means that she still spends five nights weekly in the same house with Patrick, the other two at home or in the Tube station with her husband. But it does not seem to affect Patrick now whether she sleeps in or out.

The interesting point about that story is that it does not seem to be the fact of separation from the mother to which the child reacts in this abnormal manner, but the traumatic way in which this separation takes place. Patrick can dissociate himself from his mother when he is given three or four weeks to accomplish this task. If he has to do it all in one day it is a shock to which he answers with the production of symptoms. That means that even children with the neurotic possibilities of Patrick's kind could be spared much unnecessary suffering and symptom formation by more careful handling.

April 1941

## FURTHER OBSERVATIONS

An outstanding event during this month was the big air attack on London on the night of Wednesday, 16th of April. Even for people who had gone through the period of so called

Blitz in September and October 1940, the events of this night were rather surprising and alarming. There was more gun fire than ever before, the sound of falling bombs was continuous, the crackling of fires which had been started could be heard in the distance and again all these sounds were drowned by the incessant droning of air planes which flew over London, not in successive waves as in former raids, but in one uninterrupted stream from 9 p.m. until 5 a.m.

The elder members of the staff were, of course, awake and patrolled the house, the younger members went down from their attic bedrooms and joined the children in the shelter. The children themselves, to our astonishment, slept peacefully as usual and never noticed what was going on above them.

Whether it was due to the fact that the heavy wooden beams of the shelter ceiling lessens all noise, or whether the quiet atmosphere in which they had fallen asleep carried them through the restlessness of the night outside,—the facts are that no one took notice except Patrick who sat up suddenly and said: "Gun fire."

His mother who was on shelter duty answered: "Yes, but gun fire does not hurt anybody", whereupon Patrick lay down and slept again.

Pamela woke up as usual and asked to be put on the pot but remained completely oblivious of the bombing. The two babies Graham and Roy woke once and cried for a while but since that happened nearly every night, it is difficult to determine whether it had any connection with the outside noises.

Everybody slept in the shelter after the "All Clear". The morning, of course, was different than usual. Whoever came in from the outside brought tales of damage and destruction. Our old job man who lives in a more exposed district can, on such occasions, hardly be stopped from counting corpses and revelling in lurid details to which the children like to listen eagerly.

In the garden, later in the morning, the children had occasion to watch an airplane in the sky.

An adult said: "Look, it is writing!"

A statement which Pamela corrected by saying: "Only scribbling."

None of the children seemed to connect the sight of an airplane with the idea of possible danger. Still, the children seemed rather more restless or excitable than usual as a result of the tales which they had overheard.

They were watched playing a new kind of game. Some of them climbed up on the jungle gym, and regardless of danger to those standing underneath, tried to drop a heavy iron shoe scraper onto them, which they had removed from the doorstep and carried up to the heights. When warned not to do this, they proudly asserted that this was a bomb which they were about to drop.

Little Barbara who had not been big or strong enough to join in the game, suddenly brought a handful of sand, threw it onto the others and declared it was a "gas bomb". Since the sand got into the children's faces and eyes, this game was not found to be enjoyable.

Nothing further of an unusual kind happened during the rest of the day. Also the children showed no anxiety when they were put to bed in the evening.

Only three days later, on Saturday night, when again a bigger raid seemed to develop, little Jill suddenly asked: "Are the Germans coming again?"

But she did not pursue the subject nor did fear develop.

### Identification

Iris, three years ten months old, had been sent to us originally partly because her family had been bombed out, partly because of a nervous cough which she had started soon after her father died as the result of lung trouble. When living with us her nervous symptoms came and went. Lately, she had been free from it for some time. During April she fell ill with tonsillitis. While she was in bed with a temperature, her nervous cough returned and developed into a regular attack of asthma bronchiale, with all the usual somatic accompaniments. Her tonsillitis together with her asthma disappeared within a few days. She was well for a while and then again returned to the sickroom with a slight cold aggravated by her usual nervous cough. So far we understand little about the origin and development of Iris' symptom. There is the suspicion, of course, that her cough had started in imitation of her father's cough.

The mother herself reports that a neighbour suddenly said to her: "Don't you notice, Mrs. Coster, that Iris coughs exactly the way her father did."

A tendency for hysterical identification is very evident in Iris' case. She picks up habits from the other children, adopts them as her own, drops them again after a while and picks up new ones. In the beginning, when she had formed a friendship with Barbara, a little girl of her own age, she suddenly started the same temper tantrums that had made Barbara conspicuous in the house. Though she is no thumb sucker herself, she suddenly started sucking her thumb in a way that is peculiar to Keith, a boy more than a year her junior. Her latest habit is a sort of grimacing, the origin of which, we are at the moment attempting to find among the other members of the house. It is interesting to note that during every illness, her noticeable affection for the doctor is greatly increased. This was particularly marked during the periods of asthma when the presence of the doctor helped to lessen her anxiety during attacks.

### Separation

While daily all over England more and more children are separated from their mothers and evacuated for the sake of safety, our interest is still held by the various possible results of such separations.

### Jill

We had another opportunity of observing the worst effects of sudden separation in Jill, a little girl, two and a half years old. In accepting Jill we gave in to the urging of her mother who was frightened that the child would either be infected with TB by the grandmother with whom she shared the room or with some kind of shelter disease in the very primitive place where they all spent the nights. The mother seemed rather desperate and worn out with anxiety. She begged us to let Jill benefit by the favourable conditions in our house, at least for the few weeks which she would need to find a billet in the country for herself together with the child.

Jill was a beautiful little girl, marvelously developed, sparkling with life and gaiety and seemed extremely independent for her age. It was this very independence of the child together with her evident interest in the toys, the other children and the new surroundings which decided us to fall in with the mother's wishes.

Jill was taken to the nursery where she was deep in play after a few minutes. She said good bye to her mother in a friendly way but hardly noticed when her mother left her. Only half an hour after her mother had left the house, Jill suddenly realised what had happened. She interrupted her play, rushed out of the nursery and opened every door in the house to look for her mother in the room behind it. In her running around she behaved exactly like a stray dog who has lost his master. This lasted a few minutes and then she rejoined the play-group.

These attacks of frantic search repeated themselves with ever greater frequency. Jill's expression changed, her brightness disappeared, her smiles gave way to an unusually sullen frown which changed the whole aspect of the child. It is difficult to say, of course, whether this sullenness of Jill's was completely new or whether this was the way in which she had reacted already to difficulties in her former life.

The hope that Jill with her outgoing manner would soon attach herself exclusively to some adult person in the house was not fulfilled. Her interest seemed to turn first to one of the workers in the nursery itself but before a real attachment was formed she suddenly developed a great liking for our nurse and clung to her with unexpected affection. But also this attachment had no time to ripen. Jill suddenly showed a decided preference for men, turned to all male visitors, claimed other children's daddies loudly as her own and would on evenings or Sunday afternoon sit for hours on a visitor's or fire watcher's lap, much to the men's embarrassment. Her attitude was little influenced by visits from her mother who came at times and took her out for walks. Her preference for men would indicate that her affection had turned from her mother to her father; but when, during her stay with us, her father suddenly appeared on army leave, she did not appear to treat him differently from other visitors.

Something had evidently gone completely wrong in her relations with the grown-up world. Her outstanding symptom was the continual abandoning of people she was attached to at the moment, for the sake of others who were new to her.

Whereas in Patrick's case separation from the mother had brought on a compulsive clinging to her memory, in Jill's case the result was outwardly the opposite. She lost the stable relationship to her parents which had so far governed her life, was unable to form new attachments and lived continually in search and expectation accompanied by feelings of deep discontent. We know this symptom of flight from one object to the other in adult neurotics as one of the results of early disturbances of their mother relationship.

Though Jill's symptoms quieted down and were less apparent after a few weeks, especially after a prolonged stay in the sickroom where she was surrounded by a quiet home-like atmosphere, she never regained her high spirits and bright appearance which had been her outstanding characteristics when she came.

Jill's mother found her billet in the country and took her off according to arrangement after she had been with us for eight weeks. In her case the physical advantages of being saved from shelter life were outweighed by the shock the separation from her mother meant for her. She was given no time for psychic preparation. On the one hand separation was too complete, on the other hand her stay under the new conditions was too short to make up for all the misery of adaptation.

### Hetty and Christine

The two next examples are meant to show two children under the influence of an identical situation where the handling was completely different each time.

Hetty, two years one month old, and Christine, seventeen months old, were both brought to stay while their mothers went to the hospital to be delivered of another baby.

In Hetty's case this was done with foresight and intelligent planning from the mother's side. She brought her as a day child more than two months before the expected birth of the new baby. She helped the child through a period of adaptation to daily life shared with other children which was by no means easy. Hetty was shy, at times aggressive, withdrawn and often unresponsive. She slowly accustomed herself to the nursery. A week before the expected confinement she entered the house as a boarder, slept in the shelter with the other children whom she already knew well but was rewarded in day time by frequent visits from her mother. When her mother at last disappeared into the maternity hospital, Hetty was used to her new surroundings, felt at home and showed no ill effects of any kind.

112

Christine, on the other hand was brought two or three days previous to her mother's confinement and left at once and completely though she had never before left her mother's side and had evidently been taken care of very well by her mother. She found herself unexpectedly in completely strange surroundings to which she reacted in a most bewildered way.

For days she sat or stood around quietly or crying and would only at intervals say: "Mum, Mum".

She did it in a surprisingly deep voice.

Similarly to Jill, but again in a completely different manner, she would sometimes stretch out her arms to visitors. She was at times content when she could sit on somebody's lap with her face averted. Probably she imagined herself in this position to be sitting on her mother's lap without being disturbed by the sight of a strange face.

She fell ill about a week after her arrival and reacted during her illness with apathy and listlessness. In the last week, when she was gradually getting better in the sickroom she was at last reported to have smiled and even joined in play with other children.

Again, these descriptions show that it is not the task of separation from the mother itself which is impossible to accomplish for the small child. The decisive factor for the normal or abnormal outcome seems to be the time given, which after all means the presence or absence of traumatic chock.

In this case of a nervously unstable mother and child it was certainly only the ample time given for adaptation which prevented serious outbreaks of neurotic symptoms and behaviour.

May 1941

## REACTION TO AIR-RAIDS

There were many people who felt that the great air attacks of Saturday, May 10th, were even worse than those of April 16th. Curiously enough, there was not the same state of excitement and restlessness on the day after. When our old gardener again appeared with the story of a big bomb, nobody believed him. Whether it was the feeling that we again had had a lucky escape, or whether it was that this time not one among our parents had suffered personally, the facts are that the Sunday following, the raid developed into the most peaceful day, we had experienced in the Centre. It was the first sunny springlike Sunday. Parents came and went from morning till evening, sat down to meals, or walked around our garden, watching their children at play.

Through this atmosphere of peace it slowly transpired that our old gardener had after all been right in his report. Next morning, we noticed that the neighbouring house and the street leading to it were roped off. When we questioned the police, we were told the following: there was a possibility that the bomb might still explode—in that case it would bring down the next house; ours was considered to be just outside the danger zone but on no account should we let the children go into the garden.

We were grateful to escape the great discomfort of being evacuated on the spot because it would have been none too easy to find good accomodation for 34 children at short notice. We kept the children in the house for one whole day; after that, we were offered the loan of a garden just across the street. Our children were only too happy to be released from imprisonment again and from then on the daily routine was changed to meet the new conditions. Since the weather was warm and sunny our house stayed deserted most of the time. A procession of our children was continually on its way either to or from that other garden, the older children with a weak attempt to walk in orderly fashion, the toddlers escaping in all directions and the babies being wheeled over in their baby carriages.

A bomb at a great distance may be an object of horror. A bomb, on the other hand, which settles down so near to one's own household is somehow included in it and soon becomes an object of familiarity. It is true that on the first day an unexploded bomb is contemplated with respect and suspicion. When it delays exploding, the reaction in the people around is not, as one should expect—one of thankfulness and relief. The reaction is rather one of annoyance with it which develops into contempt for the bomb as the days go by. The bomb is treated more like an impostor who has formed us into an attitude of submission under false pretences. In the end, when no one believes in its explosiveness any more, it sinks down to the position of being a bore.

Since the children know of course about this situation, we watched them closely for signs of anxiety. But in spite of the fact that most of them had been driven out of their homes by bomb explosions they did not seem to connect the idea of the bomb with the idea of possible danger.

Even Constance, nine years old, was heard to say in an angry tone: "I wish the bomb would explode so that we can use the garden again."

The nursery children were mostly impressed by the fact that our garden was closed to them. They were resigned during the first week. On the tenth day a group of them after meal time suddenly dashed for the garden entrance.

When caught and brought back, Pamela insisted: "There is no bomb".

When this was turned down, they all screamed in chorus: "There is no bomb! We are going out in the garden!"

Pamela then came in again and said firmly: "It has exploded".

This attitude of denying what is unpleasant and disturbing in reality is natural enough to children. It is more surprising that also our grown up staff was not inclined to act otherwise. Our social worker decided that this was the appropriate time to give the garden a really good overhaul. Whatever grass had survived on the children's playground was cut, a new sandpit dug, and the jungle gym repainted.

Whenever anyone tried to send a member of the staff out of the garden, he was met with the indignant remark that after all "the bomb would not go off just at this moment".

Though certainly all our windows would have been smashed if the explosion had occurred, no one in the house was ever seen to keep away from windows.

Our bomb once more became impressive when after much hard labour a bomb disposal detachment of soldiers had dug it out of its crater and loaded it on a truck to be removed. Its presence in the street, which by now had been re-opened, excited much comment among the passersby. We saw mothers lift small babies to admire it and everybody watched while the soldiers tied red silk ribbons to the rear of the car as a sign of danger in the case of collision. They sat all around it and drove off joking and singing.

When the good news that the bomb had gone was spread in the house, we again watched for reactions of relief. All we could find was an immediate desire on the part of the children to regain possession of the garden.

Charlie, four years ten months, asked with great interest whether the soldiers had driven the bomb off "in a lorry". To him the ever fascinating question of transport was more outstanding than the danger element implied. The complete reversal of all values was most distinctly shown in the way our social worker met the good news. He said: "I wish they had left it two days longer so that the jungle gym would have had time to dry."

When the soldiers returned to fill up the empty crater they were invited to have tea in our dining room where the children met them. It was at this occasion that some of the children showed definite signs of fear or anxiousness. "Fear of the bomb" was quite outside the range of their infantile emotions. "Fear of the big man" is a recognised and typical childhood fear. That the bomb meant real danger to them and the "big men" protection against it did not play a part in the situation.

Some of the children were perfectly natural, played with the soldiers, made friends with them and tried on their caps. Patrick put on an overboisterous and joking manner which he only does when he is afraid of something. Pauline and Iris on the other hand covered their eyes with their hands and could not be induced to look at the soldiers.

### Artificial Orphans

We found to our own astonishment when questioning the parents about a possible evacuation of their children to a country place that the same mothers who three months earlier refused to be separated from the children completely would be now perfectly ready to let them go. Much has been said in the newspapers, by various authorities and in the reception areas about the unreliability of mothers who will send their children to the country one day and drag them back to the bombed areas a week later. We so far have not had a single experience of this kind.

The psychic problem of the infant who has been evacuated is not easy to solve. For a child under three years of age it is extremely difficult to maintain a normal emotional relationship with an absent love object. We say in ordinary language that the small child forgets quickly. It really means that the material and emotional needs of the child cannot be satisfied from the distance. The love of the infant for his mother is closely bound up with the fulfilment of these needs. If the mother is absent, the child forms, after a short period of longing, a new relationship to a substitute mother. The relation to the real mother has become unsatisfactory and is driven from consciousness.

We can only surmise from later behaviour what changes it has undergone inside and what has become of it. Normally this period of "mourning" lasts only a very few days. After that, if the mother does not show herself again, the child settles down "quite happily". Where the psychic make-up of the child is more advanced or more complicated, adaptation takes a longer time. Some children will cling to the memory of their mother in a compulsive manner. We have given an example of this type of behaviour in the case of Patrick. Others will build up a constant phantasy of family life, put it in the place of the lost reality and work it off in play.

The most serious objection against war time evacuation of young children without their mothers is, therefore, that it produces artificial orphans. It is common knowledge that after the death of the father or mother small children behave as if their parents had just gone away. We can certainly say that when parents have only "gone away" the children behave as if they had died. This only means to say that the important factor for the small child is bodily absence or presence of the mother. The question of existence or non-existence in the real world seems to be beyond the child's emotional comprehension.

But even though, in that sense, all these little children who are separated from their parents are war orphans, the attitude of the world around is to disregard the identity of the inner psychic situation of the two kinds of children and cling to the importance of the outer reality. The child whose parents have been killed in an air-raid is an object of pity and all the difficulties that he shows seem somehow natural and are met with tolerance. The child who is only billeted in the country while his parents continue to live in London is only considered to "fret" and expected to get over it "in no time". Therefore it is precisely the study of the real war orphan and his reactions which may be of help to create a better understanding of the "evacuated" child.

## PARENTS AND CHILDREN

Since Patrick's recovery he had seen his mother almost daily or at least four or five times a week while she worked on night duty in our shelter. She had to stop her duties because of her pregnancy with a new baby and in the eighth month of pregnancy went to the hospital with varicose veins. She was immediately evacuated to the country.

Patrick, on our insistence, was permitted to see her once before she went but was, of course, unable to visit her again during the last three weeks. To our own astonishment he remained normal this time. Slight signs of anxiousness and disturbance disappeared after his one visit to the hospital. Since then he has remained perfectly normal, has not changed his behaviour or his activities in the nursery and has not shown compulsive symptoms of any kind.

The only faint traces of his former trouble are an occasional overinsistence in asking whether his "daddy is sure to come and take him out on Sunday", and a certain withdrawal of interest when his mother is mentioned by outsiders. On the other hand, he quite normally questions his father about his mother's whereabouts, is perfectly aware of the whole situation and even passes on to us reports about his

122

mother's state of health. He can now sensibly manage the same situation which made him ill before. This would be easy to understand if in the meantime he had undergone psychic treatment. Since this has not been the case, the factor responsible for the change is evidently the time factor. As stated before, he was able to digest in the course of several months the same experience which had acted on him as a traumatic shock when he had been only given a few hours to adapt to the situation.

Under the conditions in our house where children see the parents from whom they are separated fortnightly, weekly and in some cases even two or three times a week, it is instructive to follow the changes which the parent-child relationship undergoes. The first three or four visits by the mother usually have the sole effect of reproducing the shock of the original separation. The children long for the coming of the parents, greet them with all signs of pleasure, cling to them during their visit and usually burst into tears at the renewed parting. After this experience has been repeated several times the parting loses its dramatic significance and the children seem to feel certain that the mother who disappears will reappear again.

This period of o v e r v a l u a t i o n of the parents lasted, perhaps three months—with the older children three and four years of age. During the last month we entered into a new phase of the parent-child relationship. The children were still very pleased to see their parents but the time spent with them was not as greatly valued as before.

For example, Beverly's parents say: "She hardly talks to us when we take her out for a walk and whenever she sees another child she wants to run and play with her".

Rosemary's mother will sit for hours on end on her visiting days and never say a word. Rosemary dutifully stands next to her and remains as silent as her mother. As soon as her mother is gone, she revives and returns to her usual activity and endless talking. David who receives visits from his mother very often runs back to the other children afterwards as if he were afraid of having missed too much.

All this is of course the natural process of shifting affection and interest which is so well known in children of boarding school age.

Bertie
The child for whom the loss of his parents has had the most serious consequences is a little boy of now four and a half years.

Bertie's father was killed while working during an air-raid in the course of the autumn raids on London. His mother had had a complete breakdown and had been committed to a mental hospital.

Bertie is a slim, good-looking boy, very clean cut with a clear skin and delicate features. He is extremely friendly, rather gay and, in the manner of children who have spent a long time in hospitals, he does not differentiate over-much between the various grownup figures but greets everybody with an impartial smile.

While in bed he was always deep in play and would keep himself busy with a few tiny toy cars, a set of paper houses and similar play things. He never mentioned his parents and seemed so unconcerned about everything that we doubted whether any knowledge of the family tragedy had ever reached him.

After a while we had the opportunity of questioning a cousin of his mother's who visited him. We learned that Bertie did not only know of his father's death but had actually shared all his mother's grief and anxiety. His parents had been devoted to each other; his mother had never let Bertie out of her sight.

One day during the period of the big raids the father had not returned from work for his midday meal and after waiting for him for hours the mother had started the usual search. She took Bertie along wherever she went, to all the people she questioned, to the police and even in the end, to the morgue. Here he was denied admission but he waited outside while his mother found and identified his father's body. He was taken to the funeral and to the early visits to his father's grave. After that he fell ill with tonsillitis and was taken to the hospital where he came down with scarlet fever.

For his mother the separation from the child renewed the shock which she had received from the father's death. She believed Bertie dead also and began to search for him in the same frantic manner. Her psychotic attack with hallucinations followed soon after. The mother's cousin repeatedly said how good Bertie had been to his mother and how he had tried to comfort her in every way.

Since we knew the story we tried carefully to lead back Bertie's mind to his past experiences. He would now admit that his mother was in the hospital.

Certain things reappeared which he had probably been told during his hospital time: He should always eat his midday meal like his father, then he would soon be a big boy and would be taken to visit his mother.

Whenever anybody asked what he wanted to be, he would say automatically and quickly: "Big boy". When questioned about his father he said: "He is a workman who tidies away the bricks from the houses which Hitler threw down".

When the unexploded bomb was lying near the house, Bertie's mind was filled with ideas of soldiers, Hitler and bombing. He would bomb his paper houses by the hour, throw them down and carefully put them up again.

When taken to the window, he would vaguely point in some direction and say: "Look what Hitler has done".

One morning he suddenly woke in a state of great excitement. He first talked to himself loudly for awhile, then called a young nurse to his bed and told her to listen to him. From then on during the day he repeated his story to whomsoever wanted to hear it. He told how his father and other men had been at work when the bombs started to fall. They had all crowded into the underground station which was enormously strong, so strong that no bombs could hit them. Then a "puff puff train" had come and taken them all in and taken them to a place in the country where workmen were needed. They were still working there. When the war was over his father would get another "puff puff train" and come back.

Another version of the story said: In the morning his father had taken his hat and stick and his mackintosh, because it was raining. When he did not come back, he Bertie, had also taken his hat and his overcoat, put on his shoes, had gone out and had brought him home.

In addition to the story, he said his mother was not in the hospital any more. She was all well and living in the country and after the war was over, she would also get into a train and come back.

Bertie had evidently found a happy solution for the insoluble problem of his parents' fate. It is possible that all this talking represented the contents of a dream which he had had at night. But it is also possible that this story had slowly prepared itself in him in the foregoing weeks and that he had shifted and reshifted all the facts and, with the help of wish phantasies, had altered the events to his own satisfaction.

We realise that the fact of his father's death is denied from the beginning; his mother's illness which he had accepted first as a fact has also been denied. The phantasy of himself as the hero who finds his father and triumphantly returns him to the mother has originated probably at the time of his mother's search when he tried his best to comfort her.

Wherever an anxious situation arises, reassurance is immediately given by stress on the opposite fact. He tightly clenches his hands in the effort to show the strength and safety of the underground station. The fullfillment of all wishes , i.e. the reunion of the family is promised for a vague future.

Talk about these matters disappeared completely after two days. What remained was a great pleasure in playing bombing, killing and war in general, a game in which several other boys joined with pleasure.

When promised to be taken on a shopping expedition, he again awoke in the morning in great excitement and declared to several people: "My daddy is by now ready to come back".

In his thoughts, or maybe again in a dream he had mixed up the event of the shopping expedition with the expected event of his father's return. In the street he showed great fear of and interest in motor cars. He refused to cross the street whenever one is anywhere in sight. In the same way he showed a great fear of catching cold and falling ill. When on a stifling day his cardigan was taken off, he immediately ran for his overcoat so as not to "fall ill and go to the hospital".

In the shop he was very friendly with the shop assistant and told her: "I used to live in London before. But London is bombed to pieces, all the houses have fallen down and all the people are gone". London in his mind evidently stands for his past with his parents.

Lately he has had many visits from his mother's cousin who during a fortnight's holiday from work has taken him several times to her small flat. He there sees pieces of furniture which used to belong to his parents. He returns from these visits greatly agitated. He shows not the least outward sign of mourning or longing for his parents but he will sometimes during play suddenly jump up and rush aimlessly to the far corners of the nursery in a curious rabbit-like manner. Such spells of unaccountable behaviour are usually of very short duration. He will stop them just as suddenly and continue whatever occupation he was following before.

It seems certain that Bertie finds it difficult to distinguish between the manner of disappearance of his father and his mother. He probably believes that his mother is dead as is his father. This is indicated in his phantasy of their being in the country and of their returning in the same manner after the war. It is interesting to note, though, that even in his phantasy his father and mother are not together; they are kept in different places.

August 1941

## THE COUNTRY HOUSE

The children's excitement to see the country house had reached its highest pitch. Innumerable questions and remarks cropped up continually. Though no one had ever promised them cows or horses, these two animals seemed to be inseparably bound up with their idea of country life.

Charlie said whenever he felt angry: "I will hit all the cows and horses in the country house".

Pauline said: "I will jump on the cows".

Pamela asked: "Are the cows ready now"?

Whenever the children felt angry with somebody they would say: "You cannot come to our country house".

When the departure was at last announced for a definite day, Roger said triumphantly: "The war is over, peace has come and we are going to the country. But the war has lasted a long time".

His idea of evacuation did not quite coincide with ours; his desire for the advent of peace and his desire for the departure to the country house had merged into one.

On Saturday, 23 August, the children were taken out in the American ambulance and two other cars, accompanied by four adults, one dog and one canary. On arrival the children were overjoyed to see their new home, a charming, friendly modern building with all the necessary conveniences, an immense ground floor studio serving as the big nursery, two huge south rooms with bay windows for the toddlers' bedroom and playroom, a covered porch leading down to terraced lawns for perfect playgrounds, outhouses, a vegetable and berry garden and a huge orchard with three little chicken houses. The absence of horses and cows was not commented upon. The children found their bedrooms faultlessly set up and ready to be slept in, the first meal set out on their small tables and the nursery prepared with material for play and work.

Beverly said with great satisfaction after a visit to the dormitories: "I am going to s l e e p u p s t a i r s tonight and not downstairs". This meant: I am going to sleep in a proper bedroom again after eight months of shelter sleeping in a basement.

Some outstanding examples of the shock of separation are the following:

There was Mary, two years and eight months old, whose mother brought the child to the nursery so that she could take up munition work. Mary who is a gay and beautiful girl, well developed for her age, seemed at first delighted with the new experience. But when after several hours she understood that this meant separation from her mother she broke down completely, cried incessantly and was hard to quiet.

Frequent visits from the mother only seemed to aggravate her state. She formed apparently violent attachments with one teacher then with another but changed her attachments with surprising quickness. She had to hold somebody's hand continually. Since this completely put one teacher out of commission for work with other children, a substitute was invented half in earnest and half in play or joke. A skipping rope was tied around the waist of her last favourite and Mary held on to it and followed her around. This unsatisfactory state of affairs lasted for two weeks. After that time her clinging became less insistent. She allowed even her favorite teacher to leave the room at times and she began definitely to enjoy her mother's visits without bursting into tears at every new parting. Now, six weeks after her arrival, she is definitely well and settled in the house.

There was David, two years and six months old, a boy of charming, delicate appearance who in a state of fright would roll his eyes until only the whites were seen. His mother reported that he as well as his elder brother were frightened and nervous and inclined to have temper tantrums. The elder brother had for this reason been removed from several billets. He has now been admitted to the old house and sent to the country with our children. She herself was in a highly nervous state. David seemed quiet and comparatively happy in the first two days. He was inseparable from a toy dog,

Peter, whom he had brought from home. Peter slept with him, ate with him, was in his arms even when he was bathed and dressed and David insisted that Peter should be taken care of as if he were another child in the Nursery.

When his mother visited him after two days, David had his first temper tantrum, a kind of hysterical attack, in which he alternately embraced his mother, clung to her, kissed her, scolded her and hit out at her. He insistently demanded that she should kiss Peter on the mouth and hug him as if he were her baby. From then on for quite a while he reacted with temper to every imaginary insult done to Peter. He would cry whenever another child would knock against the toy and would throw himself on the floor with despair whenever the dog inadvertently fell out of his arms. Peter is evidently a symbol for himself and has to be treated as he himself wants to be treated. His mother was to make up in affection to the dog for the wrong she had done to David by sending him away from home. In David's case the difficulties caused by separation from his mother are hard to disentangle from the neurotic troubles he had certainly already shown in his life with her.

An example of the opposite kind is Sheila, three years and four months old, who entered the Nursery with a very charming little brother of two years. Sheila is a rather plain little girl who has suffered from eczema since her babyhood. She has lost her father in an air-raid and seems definitely unloved by her mother, who greatly prefers the little brother, to the girl. Sheila who is used to look after her brother and generally seems to have led the life of a miniature charwoman continued this existence in the Nursery. She would scrub the floor, wipe the tables, feed the little children and report all matters of importance to the teachers. In the middle of all these activities she suddenly discovered the joy of being a loved child herself. She developed a tender affection for the nursery superintendent and, in the middle of doing something else would suddenly run to her, throw herself into her arms and hug her. She definitely lost very little through separation from her mother and everything she meets in the Nursery is a gain for her.

September 1941

## CHILDREN IN THE COUNTRY

Since the children we sent to the country remained within their own groups and were accompanied by the staff who had looked after them for several months already, evacuation for them was no shock of any kind. It took them only a very few hours to feel acquainted with the rooms of the new house. They arrived at lunch time and at tea, their second meal in the new surroundings, no child had the slightest difficulty in finding his place at the table. The toddlers were delighted to have "real beds" again. No child seemed to miss or question the absence of a shelter.

A few weeks later, a fond memory of the shelter in Wedderburn Road seemed to wake up in them. An empty bookcase in the nursery was suddenly declared to be a doll's shelter with all the individual dolls sleeping peacefully in tiers above each other. The workers were asked by the children to crochet nets to safeguard the dolls against falling out of their beds and in this way to make the resemblance to former shelter life complete.

It took the children less than one day to get accustomed to outdoor life. They took possession of the playgrounds immediately and already on the day after arrival showed their familiarity with the lawns by standing on their heads on them and by using the space for all sorts of acrobatic stunts.

Little more than a week after their arrival in the country the children were disturbed at night by a solitary stick of bombs which dropped several miles distant. Since the noise of bombing makes itself heard in open country even more than in a city, all these Londoners—grownups and children alike—in spite of having lived through the whole period of blitz, jumped out of their beds and had quite a fright. Many of the very little children were untouched by the event. The elder children and the staff met in the hall and the corridors and some of the children needed quite a lot of quieting. The children talked for quite a while about the bombing before falling asleep again. Some of them, like Pamela quickly regained their good humour and were ready to joke. One of them said that they should write to Jimmy in London that he could come to the country now, that there were bombs there also and that he could do fire watching.

One little girl said the next morning in reporting the event: "But it w a s a kind German, he did not drop the bomb on our house".

It is rather curious to think that this is the idea of kindness with which the children of this period will grow up.

### Modes of Behaviour

One of last month's newcomers in the country house, Bertram, three years and nine months old is at varying times distressed shy, cross, affectionate and violent. He had never been separated from his mother for the first two and a half years of his life and then was taken from her very suddenly when she had to go to a hospital in the last stages of tuberculous illness. His father who knows that the mother's death is expected shortly and who is himself in the Merchant Navy brought Bertram and his elder sister to the Hampstead Nursery when on leave.

Bertram, at the beginning, spoke very little and never made any references to his past. Instead of that he would get into short fits of temper and defend himself against all sorts of harmless routine happenings with the utmost vigour but without any consistency in his behaviour. He would refuse for instance to be put to bed or to be washed or to have his throat inspected at one moment and then willingly allow to have it done the next. He would sit endlessly at table apparently finishing his lunch. The most difficult time for him was the evening when he was supposed to go to bed. On such an occasion he had one of his outbursts of anger against the nursery superintendent and assured her that he did not like her. She said simply that she was very sorry because she did like him.

He said: "I don't like you and I don't like nobody. I only like myself". Immediately afterwards he told her for the first time how his mother had gone away in a big car and had never come back again.

The evening after this conversation he did not make his usual fuss but called her to his bed and said: "Stay with me. You are my mother now."

He is now very closely attached to her, very affectionate and much easier to handle. He has succeeded in expressing the most important event in his past life in words and conscious thought and this relieves him of the necessity of expressing his memory of it in abnormal behaviour. Day after day he now adds new pieces of information about his past.

Whenever he is at cross purposes with one of the grown ups, he says threateningly: "I will put you to bed." Or "You will get no pudding".

In this way he remembers and relates the educational measures taken in the little school where he lived with his sister before they came to us. This also explains why his behaviour was always most cranky when either eating or when supposedly sleeping.

The outlet into conscious thought and speech with consequent relief in their behaviour is unluckily denied to some of our children who would be most in need of it.

We have quite a number of war orphans in our groups. Among them are two families—four children in one, two in the other—where the children have not been informed about their fathers' death. Both men were killed in air raids, the body of one has not even been recovered.

Though both mothers are competent women who immediately faced the task of going out to work to support their families, they are too much hit themselves to be able to face their children knowing and possibly talking about their fathers' death. They built up a legend of the father being "in the north of England", being "ill in hospital" and they force the children to believe in it. There is not the slightest doubt that all these six children—except of course the baby—must know all about their fathers' death. They have seen their mothers cry and have lived weeks or even months in close contact with mourning before they came to us. The mothers even take them to church at the anniversary of their father's death, to visit neighbours who condole with them; they even had to accompany the mother to the officials to debate the question of pensions, guardianship and proving of death. In spite of their emotional life being completely under the impression of their deprivation, they are denied the relief given by by talking about the matter.

One of these children, five years old, the other day broke out in the presence of the mother into the triumphant statement. "I know all about my father. He has been killed and he will never come back".

The mother answered with a fit of anger, closely questioning the child who had told her "such a lie".

The child only repeated: "You have told me yourself through your behaviour". But in the end the mother won.

She made the child repeat: "The father is in Scotland and will certainly return".

The little girl repeated the words after her with a sullen expression and had to promise never to say or think it otherwise. The children of this family show the effects of this discrepancy between the truth they know and feel and the legend they are forced to adopt in wild and unruly behaviour and general contempt for the grown up world.

The other little girl, Sheila, the little charwomen of three and a half years, reacts to every outing with her mother, especially when it takes her back to the father's world with a new excess of washing, scrubbing and looking after the other children, far beyond her years.

There is no doubt that all these children can be helped by an open discussion of their misfortune. But at the moment it cannot be done against the mothers' wishes and it will take some patient and careful work to influence the mothers to adopt this point of view.

October—November 1941

## PARENT UNDERSTANDING

From rash and inconsiderate actions of some mothers, it would be very wrong to generalise and suppose that these untaught mothers haven't understanding of their children's needs or are not appreciative also of the more subtle and complicated methods of dealing with their children. We find that the mother's own diagnosis of the child's state is very often correct.

Iris's mother for instance suggested from the beginning that the child's attacks of nervous coughing might have something to do with her father's incessant coughing in the year before his death. David's mother always knew that his bed wetting and general state of restlessness were due to her own attacks of anxiety during air raids. Patrick's mother who showed great concern and understanding about his normal state whenever he was separated from her, asked us later to take her elder girl who had developed an overly timid and frightened manner in her billet, where she was excellently well cared for in all material ways. She said it could not be good for a child to lose all confidence in her own actions in that way. She had noticed that whatever the girl did, she would stop afterwards and wonder whether she had done right.

Several mothers, who were rather doubtful of our methods in the beginning, admitted after a while that our ways of handling the children seemed more successful than theirs.

Little David's mother began to see the part she used to play in his temper tantrums and said: "It is lovely now to put him to bed without excitements".

Mary's mother on the other hand still insists that her spankings are more sensible than our indulgence when Mary is upset.

All mothers relate how much they mind when they see their children continually restricted in their activities in billets or in institutions. They are upset over the fact that in some places children are not allowed to handle freely the presents which the parents bring to them.

Bertram's and Rosemary's father, for instance, reported as one of the instances which completely turned him against their former Nursery, that a doll which he had given to his little daughter on one visit was still in the same perfect condition when he returned for a next visit after several months at sea. This, he said, could only mean that the toy had been withheld from the child and that the people in charge did not understand what a toy of this kind could mean in comforting a child separated from both parents. The child's mother is in the hospital with Tb.

Insight of this kind, in the beginning came as a surprise to us. We had rather expected the parents to wish that their presents would be respected and preserved.

Understanding of this type is shown with special clearness in a letter received last week from John's mother. John, three years old, was admitted in September to the country house. As a bed-wetter he had been handed on from one billet to another—five or six changes in all—and no further place could be found for him. He is a delicate little boy of graceful, charming appearance, friendly but non-committal, rather frightened, and lost and without emotional contact with anybody. All we could learn about him was that his father was a private in the army and that his mother was in a sanitarium with Tb. When an aunt from London visited him after a short time, we asked for particulars of his past history. She only told us that she was the mother's sister, that she belonged to a family of 13 and that she knew almost nothing about the child. But she would write and ask the mother to let us know as much as possible of the experiences the child had had all by himself during the mother's illness.

We quote the following from the mother's letter:

" . . . John hasn't had any complaints, only measles which he had last December, they lasted a week, but nothing else whatever, he has always eaten well and slept well, when John was 8 months old his daddy was called up for the Army, up till he was two years of age there was just John and I on our own so of course he had his freedom, was allowed to play in the garden, etc. and was a happy, carefree little boy, but last year we decided to go to Yorkshire to his daddy for a while, I was only there quite a short time when I had an haemorraghe, of course it came quite a shock to me when I learned what was wrong as I had felt so well, I never had the slightest suspicion of it or I should not have gone all those miles from home to leave my baby at the mercy of strangers, however, I went into the Sanatorium in December 1940 and the woman who we were staying with said she would take care of John during the time she had him his daddy used to go to see him and he said it got on his nerves to hear her keep saying to the child, "Don't do this and don't do that" and as time wore on he noticed John was being cowled down and when his daddy took him sweets he would give them to this lady and sit there and wait for her to give him one, he was never allowed to play out in the garden and when his father went on Sunday mornings to take him out she always made the excuse that he was not bathed, and then on evenings she would put him to bed just before his dad arrived, this went on for 6 months this was the period I was in the Sanatorium. I was up all day and had been for quite a while and I was feeling very well so I decided to come back to London and let some one in m yown family take care of John, and I would finish my treatment in a Sanatorium down here, but I was disappointed when I got home I found my sisters had all got government jobs and could not leave them, so I said unless I found somebody suitable I would never leave him again and it was during this time I had him that I noticed he was not the happy carefree little boy that I had left, he had altered completely, seemed to be frightened of every little thing he did, he would say "Can I do this, can I do that", he would never do anything of his own free will for fear it was wrong, I would say "yes" to everything he wanted just to get him back to his old ways, and it made me realise how very much he must have been kept down . . . I then got the chance to come to this Sanatorium and as we know some one in the country we thought it would be a good idea to ask her if she would like to have John, thinking he would have a good home and the freedom of the fields to play in, she seemed to jump at the idea of having him and she asked me to pay her 15/— a week, but I was so pleased to think that she was going to have him that I asked her to accept 18— as the cost of living was so dear and would not be much money in for her labour, this she accepted, so I came away to settle down and get better, thinking that little John was now settled and I would not have the same worry as I had before of him being tied down and watched about, but she was very particular, in the home, and I guessed that she turned out to be the same as the

146

other one, however, she wrote me a letter after a month and told me what a good little soul John was and what clean ways he had, but at the same time referring to not wanting him any longer. I never took no notice and a fortnight after I got a letter from her saying she had turned him over to a nursery with the feeble excuse that he wetted the bed, but now when I sit and think of the different places he has been to and the way he has been treated, Mrs. B . . . has done me a good turn in the long run by getting John into your nursery, now he can play with other children and do just as he pleases without somebody continually saying "Don't do this and that", so I hope he will soon get back to his jolly carefree ways as I am sure he will do by this description my sister gave me of the nursery. Well Matron, I hope I have not bored you stiff with this long letter, but I have described to you as best I can as to where John has been since my illness . . . "

Training Scheme

We have at the moment about twenty young girls of the age between sixteen and twenty-one years working for us in our houses. Apart from the very youngest they have all had some training as nurses, baby nurses, or nursery school teachers, partly on the continent and partly in England. To give a sounder foundation of some common knowledge to our work with the children, we have now decided to start out on a purely private and unofficial training scheme

147

of our own. This training scheme is strictly limited in several directions:

A   We can give no certificate at the end apart from a private letter of recommendation in cases where the young worker has been found satisfactory.

B   We spend no money on our training scheme just as we demand no fees for our children.

C   We are not able to teach everything that the curriculum of a children's nurse or nursery school teacher should include. We simply utilise whatever knowledge and experience we find among the elder members of the staff to teach the younger ones. Our task is very much facilitated by the fact that nearly all our heads of departments have in their former professional life taught either at a University, a training college or at welfare institutions.

D   The hours used for theoretical instruction were formerly rest hours for the staff which the girls were glad to give up for the purpose of learning. The practical instructions form part of the regular working day. Each girl is supposed to spend a fixed time (at least 3 months) in each department (babies, junior toddlers, nursery, sickroom. -Milk kitchen, shelter duty, kitchen and household come in for slightly shorter periods of duty.—The whole training is supposed to last for the duration of the war.

The following is the time table of this training scheme which already has begun to function during November.

## LECTURE COURSES

### THE BODY OF THE CHILD
A course of 30 lectures, to be held on Mondays, 2.15-3.15 P.M.

- A   Anatomy
- B   First Aid
- C   Nutrition
- D   Hygiene
- E   Children's diseases

### MENTAL DEVELOPMENT
A course of 16 lectures to be held on Wednesdays, 2.15-3.15 P.M.

- A   Development of the senses
- B   Intellectual development
- C   First toys
- D   An idea of testing

### DEVELOPMENT OF EMOTION AND INSTINCT

- A   An introductory course
- B   Reading seminar

### GENERAL MANAGEMENT
A course of 4 lectures to be given on Fridays, 2.15-3.15 P.M.

- A   Budget
- B   Finance
- C   The building up on an institution

# COOKING

## SEWING

Two courses of two-hour periods to alternate on Fridays after Course 4 at 2 P.M.

    A  Diet

    B  Practical Cooking (at Wedderburn Road)

    C  Practical Sewing

## GYMNASTICS

Practical demonstrations for the trainees of the respective departments.

    A  Baby gymnastics. Mondays and Thursdays, 4.30-5 P.M.

    B  Gymnastics with the Senior Toddlers, Tuesdays and Saturdays 11 A.M.

    C  Gymnastics with the Junior Toddlers, Thursdays 11 A.M.

December 1941

# REUNION AFTER SEPARATION

The Christmas holidays created special opportunities to observe certain facts about the parent-child relationship. Apart from short Sundays and occasional hours during the week there is very little chance for the parents of the Babies' Home to feel that the children really are still their own. Many of them had therefore planned a long time beforehand to take their children "home" at least for one whole day, some of them for several days at

Christmas. In many cases these hopes were disappointed through the illness of the children, in others the re-union was not as happy as the parents had expected.

Baby James's parents, for instance, had begun planning three months ago to take him home to their room for Christmas day. The father's army leave and the mother's free day from factory work coincided, which was a rare occasion. They had prepared for him a temporary crib and in all ways had set the stage for one whole day of family life. When they came to fetch him, they had to be told that he had run a high temperature the day before and though the fever was down now, it would be highly dangerous to take him out of his surroundings, to interrupt his routine and to subject him to a day's festivities. The father got very angry about it, insisted that no baby could be harmed by being taken home in a pram and that after all a cold was just a cold. The mother just stood by the crib and cried with disappointment.

But when the father, a very young boy soldier, finally stormed out of the house to get a drink, she settled down quite happily and said: "Men never understand such things," and spent the whole day in the nursery sitting with her baby.

The toddlers on the other hand went on extensive Christmas leave. Brenda, seventeen months old, was carried home in triumph in a new pink coat and leggings to her Irish mother and Indian father, both munition workers in the East end. Though she is the brightest child and has the sunniest disposition in the nursery she did not behave very graciously at home. She would not eat and this disturbed the mother who had often seen her eat enormous quantities at our place. She even took her to the doctor of the nearest Welfare Clinic to find out what was the matter.

But the doctor said with great insight: "Nothing is the matter. She is only fretting for her nurses and the other children."

The mother, who is a specially kind hearted and good natured woman said when she brought her back: "I understand Brenda. It is so dull for her at home. There is nothing she can do."

Other mothers reacted to the same experience with less friendliness. When Brian, twenty-three months old, went home he just lay down on the floor quietly, was not interested and would not play with anything. His mother was greatly worried but when she brought him back to the nursery he rushed around and was as lively as ever.

She looked at him and said: "He just cheated us."

Michael, two years and one month old, who is the greatest eater in the toddler's room would not take any food at home.

Norman's mother reported that she had to get up at four A.M. to make toast for him because he said continuously and monotonously: "I want my toast, I want my toast, I want my toast".

Kenneth, three years old, was quite content with his mother for one day. He got restless the next morning, seemed more and more disturbed in the course of the day and then towards evening said very decidedly: "And now I want to go home again to my Nelsa (Ilse, the nursery superintendent) and my nice bath".

It is naturally a bitter experience for the mothers, that after half a year's absence, these small children shift their affections and their loyalties, call the nursery their home and behave as strangers or as guests with their own parents.

We try to help this situation to the best of our ability by putting no restrictions on the visits of the parents. Still, nothing can alter the fact that children of this age can only feel fully at home in one place and will turn their affection to the people who handle them day by day. It is easier for the mother to maintain her relationship to the child unbroken than it is for the child to do the same. But just because the mother's relationship remains more or less un-altered and what is h a l f   a   l i f e t i m e   t o   t h e   b a b y   i s   o n l y   h a l f   a   y e a r   t o   h e r, the mothers cannot experience this situation without bitterness. They naturally think that it is the material comforts which the nursery has to offer, the choice of toys, the good food, the "nice bath", which has stolen the affection of the children from them. In reality, it is the extreme material and emotional dependency of the small child which forces it to form such strong ties with his immediate surroundings. For this very reason we may expect many difficult situations to arise at the end of the war when all these children are supposed to return home again.

The state of affairs with the bigger children in the Country House is quite different. Now that the quarantine has made the visits of parents impossible we have the opportunity of seeing the children under conditions which more closely resemble those of other children in evacuation. There are still some differences of course. It is astonishing that even the smaller children understand the reason why the parents have stopped coming. We encourage letters from both sides, small parcels are sent and news is taken back and forth when the doctor makes her regular visits. We find that in this distance the relationship to the absent parents is greatly idealised. Their letters are carried around and have to be read to the children innumerable times. Children who do not receive letters often get sulky and depressed.

It is interesting to note that the affection for the parents is transferred in many cases to material objects which have come as presents from the parents.

Hetty, two years and ten months old, had received a green knitted dress from her mother and went on wearing it with the greatest delight. When the dress was dirty and supposed to go to the laundry, she was upset and distressed and refused to be comforted.

In the same manner, a little toddler in Netherhall Gardens had to go to bed in high black shoes which his mother had brought him that day as a present.

Toys enjoy an entirely different valuation according to whether they are given by the nursery or by the parents. Rosemary, five years old, possesses a collection of tiny toys from her mother which she carries around, shows to everybody and calls "my very own".

Dolls given by a parent are respected by everybody as private property; dolls given by the nursery even to individual children are freely shared with everybody. Only sweets, even when sent by the parents, are shared out immediately as a matter of pride and principle.

Ronny, seven years old, who takes very little care of her clothes otherwise, looks at a little skirt made for her by her mother and says: "I won't wear it to school. Only for best."

This transference of affection from the parents to their presents can sometimes go quite beyond the limits of normal reactions. Bertie, four years old, for instance who has never overcome the shock of separation from his mother, a bad case of hospitalized Tb. and from his father who is a sailor on the ocean, has developed a craze for parcels, since parcels are the one connecting link between him and his absent mother. He does not care about the contents; he just demands that all his old toys be wrapped up as parcels and given to him to open. As soon as he has opened them he wants them wrapped up again. His continual and never satisfied wish to return to his mother cannot express itself in words. It has disappeared from consciousness and instead expresses itself in this compulsive wish to open parcels.

January—March 1942

## ARTIFICIAL FAMILIES

We have recently adopted a new arrangement of work with our nursery children in Netherhall Gardens which influences their life in a decisive way. Since these children receive frequent visits from their own mothers, we had expected that they would not be searching for real mother substitutes and could be satisfied with more impersonal and diffuse attachments to the various nursery workers dealing with their group. We had not assigned special children to special workers nor divided the group for other purposes than the practical ones of play, graded according to age. All the children knew all the workers in their group and were handled by them indiscriminately for the purposes of bathing, dressing, going for walks etc.

There were two factors which decided us to change this arrangement. The one was that certain children suddenly showed strong preference for certain workers, followed them about, did not want to be separated from them and demanded attention of a very personal nature. Since the workers felt that no favoritism should be shown, this led to all sorts of disappointments and denials for the children. The second factor was that certain steps in development were slow in coming; that in spite of all opportunities provided, certain children were reluctant to grow out of their baby habits and others took too long in overcoming reverses in their development due to separation from home. We attributed these difficulties to the lack of a stable mother-relationship.

The step taken was the subdivision of the large nursery group into six small "family groups", of about four children. In assigning the children to their new substitute mothers, we followed the signs of preference shown on the one hand by the children, and on the other hand by the young workers. Each "mother" now has more or less complete charge of her family. She alone bathes and dresses her group, is responsible for their clothes and offers them protection against all the current mishaps of nursery life. There is no necessity any longer to refuse a child special attention of a motherly kind.

The result of this arrangement was astonishing in its force and immediacy. The need for individual attachment for the feelings which had been lying dormant, came out in a rush. In the course of one week all six families were completely and firmly established. But the reactions in the beginning were far from being exclusively happy ones. Since all these children had already undergone a painful separation from their own mother, their mother-relationship is naturally burdened with the effects of this experience. To have a mother means, to them equally, the possibility of losing a mother; the love for the mother being thus closely accompanied by the hate and resentment produced by her supposed desertion. Consequently, the violent attachment to the mother substitutes of their own choice was anything but peaceful for the children. They clung to them full of possessiveness and anxiety when they were present, anxiously watched every one of their movements towards the door of the nursery and would burst into tears whenever they were left by them for a few minutes.

Jealousy developed alongside with the mother-attachment. There were two types of jealousy to be seen; one directed against the children of the same family group who actually shared the attention of the mother substitute; or when the children succeeded in accepting these brothers and sisters who were forced on them, they directed the full impact of their jealousy against the children outside their family group and would not allow their worker to have any dealings with them. For a while we really thought that our grand innovation had been a great mistake. The formerly peaceful nursery reverberated with the weeping of children whose "mother" had left the room, for instance to get something from the next room, and whose absence was mourned as if she would never return. Fights among the children multiplied in frequency and intensity.

Luckily, this state of affairs did not last longer than two to three weeks. With the realisation that their new mother substitute really belonged to them, reappeared as often as she disappeared and had no intention to desert them altogether, the state of frenzy subsided and gave way to a quieter, more stable and comforting attachment. At the same time, the children began to develop in leaps and bounds. The most gratifying effect was that several children who had seemed hopeless as far as the training for cleanliness was concerned, suddenly started to use the pot regularly and effectively.

Bathing times in the evening have now become times of special intimacy when each child is certain of the full and undivided attention of its favourite adult. This again, has had a remarkable effect on the development of speech. All the children in the group have greatly enlarged their vocabulary. And several children who were rather backward in their speech development due to nursery life, have now, under the influence of this new stimulus made up for these arrears.

There is every hope at the moment that the speech of all the children will reach the level of development which it would have attained under the conditions of home and family life.

Real families, as for instance the three Fitzgibbon and the two Miles children, were of course left together in our family groups.

There is the possibility that these newly formed attachments might have consequences for the relationship of the children to their visiting real mothers. Curiously enough no signs of such changes have so far appeared on the surface.

The occurrences in this group are at the same time a clear demonstration of the known fact that children transfer their early relationship to their families onto all the people who later play an important part in their lives. This transference of feeling is responsible, on the one hand for the stormy and conflicting nature of the attachment of the child to the nursery worker, for the mixture of love and hate, possessiveness and jealousy. It explains, on the other hand, why the consequences of such attachments are so far reaching where education and development is concerned. With the full return to the type of attachment which had been interrupted by the separation from the family, the child resumes his steady progress towards the formation of a normal personality. He overcomes his childish habits and there unfolds the functions which belong to that particular stage of his individual development.

## CONFLICTING ATTITUDES

Our attempts to start "artificial families" in our nursery, i.e. to assign three or four children only to one young worker as their special "mother" interested some of our readers and led to further discussion of the subject. This again was a welcome opportunity to review once more our observations about the attitude of the real mother towards the child which is separated from her and the reactions of the child to the expressed or unexpressed emotions of the mother.

In trying to trace the numerous failures of the billeting system to their sources, a great deal of attention has been paid to the attitude of the foster mothers, and to the difficulties of the children which often seemed to make the task of foster mothers an impossible one. Less has been said about the inner attitude of the mothers themselves. But it remains a fact that children are taken out of billets and nurseries and brought back to danger areas even where billets and nurseries are satisfactory and when the children themselves are perfectly easy to handle. They are taken home in a great number of cases because the mother cannot cope with the conflict within her own feelings. Her conscious wishes for the safety of the child contrast with other, only dimly perceived or wholly unconscious feelings, which lie at the basis of the mother-child relationship.

## Ambivalent Attitude of Mothers towards Separation from their young Children

We generally over-estimate the strength of the mother's sensible wish to have the child removed from danger. Even in the middle of air raids a mother may show a double reaction in this respect. She wishes to have her child well out of danger, but at the same time to keep it near her, where she can personally care for it, watch over it and can know just where it is at the moment. She feels no one could protect her child as she can and therefore feels reassured by its presence. Reason and emotion definitely work against each other at these times. This may explain some of the continuous "to and fro" of evacuation. While one wish of the mother is active in sending the child to the country, another,, purely emotional one, is the agent to bring it back again to her side.

## Expression of the same Ambivalence on Visiting the Child

When the mother visits the child she will come with her emotions of longing, augmented by the doubt and worry whether she has done the right thing for the child. It would gratify her in one way to find that the child is worse off away from her than with her and therefore she will be very ready to find fault and will examine the child for signs of neglect and ill-treatment and will observe the nurses or foster mother with critical eyes. On the other hand she, of course, wants to find her child well and content. A sensitive child, besides having its own emotional reactions will feel this tenseness and conflict in the mother. It will be aware of her critical attitude and feel torn between its aliegiance to her and the incipient liking for his new surroundings.

These emotions which exist as under-currents during the whole length of the visit then create violent disturbances when the time for leave-taking arrives. This is generally a most painful experience for the mother as well as for the child. The child will cling to the mother, scream and show its misery in a noisy manner. The mother would certainly not want her child to let her leave gladly but she cannot stand these upsetting scenes. She reacts to them, by trying, on her next visit either to fool the child by pretending that she is not leaving when she really intends to do so or by saying goodbye to the child over and over again. After a mother has experienced such scenes repeatedly she will acquire a new conflict: she feels that her visits only add to the unhappiness of the child and she is now torn between the desire to stay away so as to spare the child further unhappiness and the desire to reassure herself by coming to visit the child again as soon as possible.

The situation is, naturally, even worse for the mother if the child reacts to her coming and going with apparent indifference. She is unable to understand such unfaithfulness, she will be hurt, jealous, unhappy and probably will lengthen the intervals between her visits. She suspects the people who take care of the child of "turning it against her". Mothers in this state will at one moment be cross, at the next over-affectionate with their children. If not helped over this difficult moment, the most likely way out for them will be to take the child home again.

In the Hampstead Nursery we avoid the worst of these complications by keeping open house for the mothers. They are reassured by the feeling that they have easy access to their children, that their visits are no disturbance to the routine of the household, that they can take their children out for walks and home for nights whenever they are free. Nothing which goes on in the nursery is hidden from their eyes so that their worst suspicions are allayed.

But even with the best intentions these conditions cannot be always kept up. We went through a difficult time when the country house was in quarantine for scarlet fever and had to be closed to visitors for three months. Mothers who, under ordinary visiting conditions, felt very placid about their children's stay with us, would suddenly call up by telephone in an excited manner, complain that they had not received an answer to some imaginary letter of theirs which had never reached us, that they "worried day and night" about their child, that they "did not even hear whether the child was alive or dead", etc. Several mothers took their children home on visits after the lifting of the quarantine to make up for lost contact. But these visits did not prove too satisfactory. Some mothers complained that the children did not seem the same to them, one of our stoutest girls was considered too thin by the mother.

Little Sandra, three years old, refused to look at her father whenever he tried to approach her, whereupon he telephoned us in an excited manner and declared: "I do not like the goings-on in that country house".

But fortunately Sandra cried at the parents' next visit when the moment of parting arrived. That, completely helped the situation and restored her father's confidence in us.

A great many of these reactions of the parents is fully conscious. The mothers specially are well aware of their double feelings. They would like to have their children stay with us in safety and under favourable conditions and yet they would also like to have them home again. They are also aware that it is the changed behaviour of the child which upsets them and strengthens the wish to have it return home. What they do not realise, however, is that the criticisms on which they pretend to base their decisions are unreal or displaced, and that the child's reactions are often increased by the conflict in the mother's mind.

In the long run even these irrational factors in the parents are open to influence. The pride in the development of the child, its concrete gains in health and knowledge, the loss of bad habits are very real factors in deciding the outcome of the conflict.

### Undisturbed Positive Reactions of Mothers to their Babies, even after Separation

In Netherhall Gardens, there is good opportunity to observe the various attitudes of visiting mothers to their small babies. Here the mothers know when they leave their babies that even with frequent visits they cannot expect recognition from them before they are a few months old. Some mothers visit daily, some weekly and only a few less often. There are certain very natural, very possessive mothers who behave in much the same way on their visits. They enter the room and make straight for the cot where their baby is lying. They immediately pick it up and handle it in the most confident manner.

One mother of twins for instance placed the children with us when they were four months old. They have now been with us for a period of nine months and during that time she has never failed to visit them daily in her off hours from work. At times our nurses were shocked at her apparent rough treatment of them. They worried, as time went on, why she did not learn something from their much quieter handling of babies. This mother seizes one twin after the other out of her cot, hugs it, holds it firmly in her hands and squeezes it. Both children react to this rough handling with evident pleasure. Now that they are older she even slaps them to the horror of the nurses. But the twins show more contact with the visiing mother than with the nurses who are constantly with them. This is shown very clearly at their feeding time. Whenever a nurse feeds one of the twins, the other waits more or less patiently in its bed. But when the mother is feeding, the twin who is kept waiting screams and makes impatient noises all the time to call the mother's attention. There is no doubt about its jealousy. The rough treatment given by the mother is rightly interpreted by the children as an expression of her possessive love.

A similar situation can be observed in another baby who entered the nursery at the age of six and a half months. He had been in unsatisfactory billets for four months, was taken home by the mother and came to us after three weeks of home life. The mother is a huge woman, extremely pleasant, a most motherly type with an immense lap. The baby felt ill after its arrival and the mother could not visit for the entire first week because her husband at home had fallen ill as well. When she came at last and found him with a bad cold she was worried, she picked him up, cuddled him, crooned over him, rocked him, rather jerked him back and forth, held him very close and finally soothed him to sleep. She put all the emotions which she had withheld from him during this week of separation into this short space of time. There is no doubt about it that some of her feelings imparted themselves to him. When she came a fortnight later he seemed very shy with her, felt strange and did not recognise her until she held him again tight in her arms and crooned and rocked him as she had done before. He then cuddled down and was a real picture of contentment.

The same feelings can also be expressed in a completely different manner. We have a Free French baby, who entered the nursery at the age of ten weeks. Her parents visit regularly once a week and nearly always together. They lean over the child's cot, handle her delicately and adoringly, somehow afraid to touch her except in the most gentle manner. Now, that the baby is ten months old, her mother has a certain way of sitting on a chair with the baby on her lap facing the father who often feeds her in that position. Also this worshipping attitude of the parents surely makes some lasting impression on the child.

Anyway this possessive handling as well as the adoring one certainly goes far in outweighing the comparatively unemotional, even and gentle treatment which the children receive from the nurses who take care of them.

### Ambivalence towards Babies

All baby-mothers mentioned so far are very motherly types, possessive, affectionate, sure of themselves and in no way torn by conflicting emotions in regard to their babies. But there are other mothers who, in contrast to them show the well known signs of double feelings towards their children.

A good example of this type is Sandy's mother who brought the baby to us when she was twelve days old. At first she visited regularly every week, then she began to come less often. When the child was four months she did not appear for several weeks and when she came again she failed to recognise her baby. Sandra had lost a lot of her black hair in the meantime. She would only believe that the child was really hers after inspecting all the other children in their cots. After this visit she again stayed away for several weeks. When she visited next she went straight to the cot, probably in order to prove to herself and to us that she knew her baby. She picked Sandra up, hugged and kissed her but Sandra did not like it and shrieked with terror. It took hours to quiet her again. While the nurse was holding her and trying to calm her, the mother paced up and down the room looking tense and worried. Every time she approached, the baby started shrieking again. It was quite evident to us that the child reacted to the mother's violent emotion. The next time the mother came, after barely a week, she approached Sandra's cot very quietly; she did not try to kiss her or to pick her up but played with her as she lay there and Sandra seemed quite contented.

The mother's feelings on those visits are not difficult to discern. Sandra is an unwanted and illegitimate baby, the mother's interest in her is uncertain and unreliable in the highest degree.

Her unconscious wish against the baby betrays itself in the failure to recognise the child. The child felt this negative emotion and reacted with terror. On the other hand there is also conscious love and affection which impel the mother to visit her and determine her reactions to a certain degree.

### Purely Negative Reactions towards the Baby

The situation is much less involved where the mother only has the straight and undisturbed wish to get rid of her child. An example of this was Johnny whose mother delivered him to us at the age of three weeks. We had no vacancy at the time but accepted him since it was evident that the mother would otherwise leave him on the next doorstep. She weaned him immediately and left the same day against all urging to stay at least a few days. She visited a few times and then stopped. The next news came from an Adoption Society with whom the mother had made arrangements already before his birth. In this case it seemed quite impossible to detect any conscious or unconscious leanings in the mother towards the child.

## Summary

Observations of this kind may be useful in explaining some of the puzzling behaviour of mothers during the evacuation of their children. With the recognition of unconscious wishes and their conflict with conscious attitudes "puzzling behaviour" usually can be explained as an unsuccessful attempt to combine an expression of both sides in one action or to satisfy the two attitudes, one after the other, in two sets of actions.

Under the conditions of normal and legitimate family life the only feelings towards the child of which the mother is conscious are positive feelings of pride of possession, love and affection. It is true that every mother also has emotions of another nature. The baby is also a burden to her, sometimes a disturbance in the relationship to the father, sometimes felt as a threat to her own body, sometimes a disturbance in enjoying herself etc. But under favorable conditions feelings of this kind are usually barred from consciousness. Wherever they appear on the surface as impatience or exasperation with the child, outside reasons are found to explain their existence. In this way we get an interplay in the mother between conscious positive feeling and repressed negative feelings towards the child. The unconscious feelings may remain dormant under the conditions of normal family life. When mother and child are forcibly separated, as for instance for the purpose of evacuation, the mother may suddenly feel the separation as a fulfillment of her unconscious desire to get rid of her child. In that case she will be unable to stand the situation. She will disregard all reasons against it, will use the slightest pretexts to explain her decision to herself and will enforce re-union with the child so as to be re-assured about her own love for it.

Under unfavorable social and economic conditions and with unwanted illegitimate children the emotional situation of the mother is completely reversed. Her entire conscious mind is filled with the desire not to have the baby before it is born or to get rid of the child after its appearance. Instinctive motherly feelings towards the child cannot fail to be present as well, but they are felt as a threat to the mother's own existence and therefore banned from consciousness. Here the conscious wish of the mother and the necessities of evacuation coincide.

Mothers of this kind present no difficulty in the beginning of evacuation. Their attitude only becomes a danger when they fail to visit, completely lose touch with the nursery or billet where their children have been placed and will certainly be untraceable when their children are supposed to return home at the end of the war.

But also with mothers of this type the unconscious attitude, in their case the positive one, has to be reckoned with and can be brought into play by change of circumstances. When the mother's hostility has been expressed in the initial separation from the child, when further, the economic threat which the child means to her has been removed through the outside help represented by the billet or nursery, the motherly feelings can in their turn rise to consciousness. Since under the new conditions they meet no condemnation from the conscious personality of the mother, it is sometimes possible against all expectations to establish good relations between these mothers and their children just under the conditions of nursery life.

August—December 1942

# CHILDREN'S REACTIONS TO WAR

There were only two daylight alarms and one night alarm in London during the last month. Neither the day nor the night routine were much disturbed by them. In obedience to the warnings issued by the government we keep up all precautions, which means that all children continue to sleep in the shelter dormitory with exception of those who are kept upstairs because of whooping cough.

The Country House had one night full of excitement. A German aeroplane dropped bombs in the neighborhood and was chased by British fighters. There were flares and guns and everybody listened to the fight. All the younger children slept through the noise but most of the older ones were awake and anxious and needed soothing.

### Children's Reactions to Bombs

The following stories record some recent sayings of our children concerning the subject of war.

After three years of war the idea of fighting, killing, bombing etc. had ceased to be surprising or extraordinary. The existence of these activities is now accepted by the children as an essential part of their picture of the world.

There are still some little ones to whom war means nothing, for example—Hilde, three and a half years old, who looks up into the sky and says: "Looks at the nice aeroplane, I'd like to have it for Xmas." But even at this age such lack of understanding is exceptional.

David, three and a half years old, complained when the alarm was given in the last daylight raid: "The sirens are eating me up." The remark shows his sensitiveness to the sound which, also for many adults, holds something of the threat contained in the howling of a wild animal.

His friend Dick of the same age explains in answer: "The sirens are in the balloons" which sounds like a reminder of the many theories about the hole of the balloons which many adults also held at the beginning of the war.

Whenever new alarms occur the older children come out with memories of past experiences.

John, six years old, related one evening: "After the last war there was one street where my aunt lived and there were no houses left, all are bombed, only the house of my aunt is left. And now they build new houses." The term "after the last war" refers in the children's language to the period of the blitz before John came to us.

Also Janet, five years old, likes to speak about her past experiences. She says: "Once there dropped a bomb next to our house and we had no shelter. So we all had to lie on top of each other. First was my little sister, then I, then my mummy and daddy. I did not like it at all." Then she continues, smiling:

"Do you remember the first night here when we all were so noisy that the Germans dropped a bomb on our house? But it was so very far away. Do you know it still?"

Janet's first part of the story is probably a correct report of what had happened to her nearly two years ago, when she and her family had their house destroyed above them. The second part of the story contains a mixture of real and imaginary elements of what happened last year. A stick of bombs was actually dropped not on, but in the neighborhood of the Country House and not on the first night, but a little more than a week after the arrival of the children there. This is a good example of a child's interpretation of such a happening. In Janet's mind the bomb was dropped as punishment because the children were too noisy. Her smile and the contradiction in the story itself "on our house, very far away"— prove that Janet is herself well aware of her own additions to the truth.

She herself had at the time commented, with evident relief, after the raid was over: "It was a kind German, he did not drop the bomb on our house."

Though this sounds like a rather alarming new conception of kindness—to drop bombs on other people's houses only—it means to Janet something completely different; the German bomber had, in her conception, behaved as she had known her parents to behave often; he had threatened punishment, had frightened her, but in the end had not carried out the threat.

The night raid over the Country House produced an anxiety attack on John, six and a half years old. He is a typical example of anxiousness in a child due to the nervousness of the mother. His mother had developed anxiety states during the raids, had never gone to bed while an alarm lasted, had stood at the door trembling and insisted on the child's not sleeping either. John, then five years old, had to get dressed, to hold her hand and to stand next to her. At the time he developed extreme nervousness and bed wetting. He had quickly improved after separation from his mother and not shown any unusual behavior in raids.

Now after an interval of more than 18 months he has attacks of anxiety which definitely resemble those of his mother in all details. During the last raid, he woke up, was frightened, trembled and looked pale.

He said: "I don't like bombs, why do they drop bombs? Where are the children?" He was taken out of bed and shown the children. "Where is Irene? Is Bertie in bed, Is Georgie asleep? I want to see him!" When back in bed he suddenly whispered: "Is big John still alive?"

When asked why he worried about this, John said: "I saw his face."

He meant he imagined seeing his face; John was not in the room in reality.

He continued to ask: "Is Sophie in the kitchen?"

After the all clear he still wanted to be told what was going on outside. When he learned that British fighters had been hunting a German plane, and had probably got it, he was not relieved.

His worries finally transferred themselves to the German pilot. "I would not like to see a dead man, would you?" When told that the German airman might have been taken prisoner and not killed he protested: "He is not an air-man, he is a Ger-man." For John, there are probably two very different kinds of men, one good, one bad and not to be confused with each other.

After the night described above, for instance, all the bigger children talked about the attack on their way to school.

Only Katrina, eight years old, skipped along happily in front of the others and related a conversation she had just had with an old gentleman, whom the children met every morning: "He said: 'Lovely morning' and I told him School is nice again." Katrina reports this and runs off again.

Mary, ten years old, the eldest girl of the house shakes her head moodily at such gaiety.

She says: "I do think Katrina forgets that there's a war on."

An absolutely practical and matter of fact comment was made the same morning by Janet, five years old.

She said: "What is the good of the Country House? They drop bombs in London and they drop bombs in the Country."

## Children's Reaction to Hitler

An endless subject for talk which never fails to excite the imagination of the bigger children is Hitler's badness. The figure of Hitler is vivid to them not as that of a powerful enemy but as the incarnation of evil, i.e. a new edition of the devil.

They never talk about the British fighting against the Germans but of a conflict between God and Hitler. They are at the age when their own conflicts between good and bad are very vivid to them, when at one moment they are completely "bad" and at the next swing over to "goodness" and intolerance of the small misdeeds of the younger children. These inner conflicts form the basis of their interest in world affairs. Katrina, eight years old has a restless evening and starts a long conversation before falling asleep.

181

She says: "Teacher says there are angels and once when we were in an air raid shelter the Germans dropped bombs on us and we were very frightened. There was a lady in the shelter and she said there is a man sitting in heaven and he puts his arms out and he hides the people so that the Germans cannot bomb us. It is God. No German can do anything to us. Who made God? Who made everything? How did everything start?" She settles down to sleep but after a few minutes she is heard to laugh quietly to herself and then she whispers: "Could God get wicked one day? Wouldn't it be funny if God would get wicked and Hitler good?"

It is easy to see that her own thoughts about God come from another source and have little or nothing in common with the teaching she receives in school and the religious consolation heard in the shelter.

John, six and a half years old, worries about the same problems.

After the groups of school children has disturbed the younger ones with their noise he asked: "Why are we naughty? Who tells us to be naughty?" and then smiling, "God tells us to be naughty!" When somebody answered that this could surely not be so, John said promptly "But he made the Germans. Why did he make them nasty Germans?"

The same question of responsibility, this time not for the naughtiness of the children but for the outbreak of the war is repeated in another conversation between John and Katrina.

John says: "I think God said to Hitler that there should be a war."

Katrina answered quickly and angrily: "Oh, no John."

John notices that he has said the wrong thing, is frightened and asks Katrina very humbly, "What *did* he say then?"

The same idea of God being responsible for everybody good or bad is reflected in another conversation between Mary and Peggy and Katrina.

They ask: "Whom will God help to win the war, Hitler or us?"

Before anyone else can answer, Katrina answers: "God will help both Hitler and us, because he likes all people."

On the other hand, this idea of bad people being liked is insupportable to other children.

Marion in a happy mood on the way home from school sings a little song of her own, "I like my Georgie and I like my Alice and I like everybody, everybody is good!"

Janet interrupts her: "You don't like everybody, you don't like Hitler."

Marion this time is too happy to argue it out. She says simply: "But Hitler is so far away." Which means at this moment her mind is not troubled by the dangers of badness.

These stories only record thoughts of the children about one special subject. Their minds are equally busy with the difficult questions of death, birth, marriage and religion. They even become conscious of the fact that they are thinking.

Janet who is always the most explicit, remarked the other day: "Whenever I think, I think with my head, isn't it funny."

# CONCLUSIONS

Why are wartime nurseries so difficult to run? Do so much more thought, energy and money have to be spent on them than seemed necessary in former times?

Nursery Schools have always been planned as extensions of the home. They provide space where the home is overcrowded, safety where kitchens or streets are dangerous to play in, toys to be handled where family possessions have to be respected, and attention and interest from the nursery teacher where mothers are overworked and harassed. This was true of the proletarian nurseries in Middle Europe and in Russia. In America, on the other hand, where nurseries for the middle classes are no less frequent than elementary schools, they provide the community life for which the child is ready, and which the small middle class family is unable to give.

In none of these cases were Nursery Schools meant to substitute for the home, no more than a free milk scheme in schools is meant as a substitute for home cooked meals, than welfare clinics do away with the need for the mother's care, or child guidance clinics with the need for educational efforts on the part of the parents. All these services were simply extensions of the home, and they worked best when allowed to function each as one link in a chain of public services for child welfare.

We are all conscious of the fact that our present situation is widely different. Families are dissolved, homes hardly recognizable as such, many children scattered in billets, many clinics closed. The Nursery schools, where they exist, find themselves suddenly confronted with the task of filling all these gaps, of fulfilling all the functions of child welfare rolled into one. In wartime, the nursery, even if not residential, becomes a foster home. Since most children have gone through long waiting periods before admittance to a nursery, they are harmed in some way by the war conditions. That means that the nurseries have to admit children in weakened bodily condition, for instance, shelter sleepers of twelve months standing. They admit children who are shocked not so much by bombing, as by shelter life and war conditions in the family. Which means that, besides their program of ordinary education, they have to fulfill the functions of a convalescent home and school for problem children. Such tasks can be taken over wherever the doctor, the psychologist, teacher and nurse combine forces. It is, perhaps, not widely enough recognized that the most difficult of these various tasks is to lessen the shock of the breaking up of family life, and to find—during the absence from the mother—a really good substitute for the mother relationship.

In this respect also many nursery schools have tried to do their best. Attempts have been made in many places to break up larger groups into smaller ones; to assign no more children to one worker than would be natural in an ordinary family; to let, as far as possible, the same workers always handle the same children. I do not think that these attempts, necessary as they are, have been completely successful. In residential nurseries, especially, no planning of this kind does away with the fact that workers need off-hours during the day, off-days during the week, and have to have the nights to themselves. The mother relationship in these early stages, on the other hand, is based on a twenty-four hour attendance to the child's needs. Many children of two, when entering the nursery have never been separated from their mothers for one day or night. Also— workers are not tied to their jobs as mothers are tied to their children. Wherever we base nursery work purely on the personal tie between the individual child and the individual worker, we prepare the way for possible new shocks of separation, and for repeated disappointments.

I have seen other nursery schools despair of these attempts. Instead of creating mother substitutes, they try to lay greater stress on the new and positive elements of nursery life itself. After all, the child gets more companionship and social life than he would at home. And what is lacking in mother's love might be given in a general atmosphere of friendliness and affection, in intelligent care and better educational efforts than the untaught mother would have been capable of.

I have seen astonishingly few attempts made to include the real mothers themselves in the life of the nursery. There are very few nurseries where mothers' visits are welcome, where efforts are made to bring home routine and nursery routine into one line. The danger evidently is not realised that the child who goes back and forth between home and nursery may, in the end, feel strange in both places. Even in residential nurseries no material help is given to make mothers' visits more frequent; nor to provide facilities to lengthen the duration of such visits.

I once tried to explain to an official visitor why the nurseries I am connected with spend a good deal of time and planning on parents' visits, and gladly suffer every disturbance of routine to make the parents take their share in the life of the nursery. My visitor said that, after all, the children could not have everything. "You can't have it all nice in a war." This evidently means that when the other needs of the child are provided for, love from the parents is a luxury. It is certainly nice for the child to have it, only wartime has temporarily done away with that luxury as it has with others.

I had heard this same remark applied during the last war, referring to material things like sugar, fresh fruit and butter, of which continental children were deprived. At that time these things were considered luxuries. Since then, they have been recognized as body building materials. Today, all efforts are made to provide children with sugar and vitamins; everybody is afraid of the consequences caused by deficiencies in this respect. At some later date, when knowledge of the psychic needs of the child is more wide-spread, we shall be just as frightened at the thought of the deficiencies in the child's psychic development whenever necessary elements, like the "mother relationship," are insufficiently existent in his early youth.

Today the knowledge that certain types of mental maladjustment always coincide with the lack of an ordinary home life in the first five years, is still restricted to a few psychiatrists and phychologists.

The mother relationship of the small baby is still comparatively simple. The relationship is one-sided; the mother gives and the child receives. At that time it seems comparatively easy to exchange the person of the mother for another one—if this person takes over completely.

But this primitive form of love relationship changes before the end of the first year. On the basis of the "stomach love" the child develops a real attachment to the person of the mother. This new love of the child is personal, exclusive, violent, is accompanied by jealousies and disappointments, can turn into hate and is capable of sacrifice. It is directed first towards the person of the mother, slowly includes the father, takes notice of brothers and sisters in various ways, and leads the child into all the complications of early emotional life. If, at the height of this development, the child is suddenly removed from all the people signficant for him, he goes through a short period of mourning. All his personal ties are broken. But since he is helpless and absolutely dependent on the strangers who now take care of him, he is thrown back once more into the former primitive stage of "stomach love". He reacts once more like a baby, i.e. at best to material comforts with material contentment.

The emotional relations of the small child to his parents are of importance for his development in two main respects: One, that this childish love is the pattern for all later love relationships. The ability to love—like other human faculties—has to be learned and practiced. Wherever, through the absence of or the interruption of personal ties, this opportunity is missing in childhood, all later relationships will develop weakly, will remain shallow. The opposite of this ability to love is not hate, but egoism. The feelings which should go to outside objects remain inside the individual and are used up in self-love. This is not what we want to produce.

The second aspect is of equal importance. It is this first love of the child which education makes use of. Education demands from the child continuous sacrifices. The child has to give up his primitive habits, to become clean, to lessen his aggression, to restrict his greed, to renounce his first sexual wishes. He is ready to pay this price if he gets his parents' love in return. If such love is not available, education either has to threaten or to drill or to bribe—all methods unsatisfactory in their results. Our educational success in the war nurseries, therefore, will largely depend on whether we can succeed in creating, or conserving for the children, their proper emotional relationships with the outside world.